*Prayer Our Glorious Pri*
friend, Pastor Chuck Sn
not only the greatest gift of eternal life through salvation in
Christ, we receive the blessed Holy Spirit as our guide and
counselor.

With great clarity Pastor Chuck writes about the honor we have
to approach the throne of grace and mercy through prayer. He
masterfully teaches the principles of praying to God the Father
and emphasizes the power that is ours when we rely on the
Holy Spirit to guide and nurture our prayer lives. I encourage
all believers to study Pastor Chuck's book based upon biblical
principles.

Franklin Graham
President and CEO
Samaritan's Purse
Billy Graham Evangelistic Association

I have read several books on prayer but I can honestly say that
this book changed my life. It changed how I viewed God and
approached Him; it changed how I regarded prayer and how
often I frequented God's throne.

I am so grateful for Chuck Smith's insights from Scripture and
the transparent examples from his own personal life. It's evident
that Chuck not only knows the Bible but knows its Author inti-
mately. This book is a *must* for every believer who desires to
grow closer to God's heart.

Pastor Skip Heitzig
Calvary Chapel Albuquerque, NM
Author of *When God Prays*

The importance of prayer is unsurpassed in the Christian walk. Yet if the truth were told, a lot of believers walk around with a lot of questions about prayer—what is it, why is it so important, how does it work, and when does it practically pertain to my life?

Pastor Chuck's years of experience in both the pulpit and the prayer closet qualify him to answer these pressing questions for us, which he does with his distinct wisdom and grace in *Prayer Our Glorious Privilege*. This is a book that the believer can't afford to miss out on, and it's a privilege to recommend it.

Pastor Bob Coy
Calvary Chapel Fort Lauderdale, FL

Very often books addressing the subject of prayer can leave you with the impression that an effective prayer life is hopelessly complex and unattainable. Here is a book on prayer that you will not only begin to read, but finish reading, containing instruction that is biblical, clear, and immensely practical regarding this blessed part of the Christian life.

Pastor Damian Kyle
Calvary Chapel Modesto, CA
Author of *Our God is a Blessing God*

One of Chuck's greatest gifts, to me, has always been to communicate the relational aspect of our faith. It is refreshing in such a complicated contemplative, method-oriented world, to just enjoy prayer as our glorious privilege. By the blood of Christ, a way has been opened up for us to approach our Father in a childlike simplicity.

Thank you, Chuck, for your unwavering commitment to the faith once delivered to the saints.

Pastor Joe Focht
Calvary Chapel Philadelphia

# PRAYER

## OUR GLORIOUS PRIVILEGE

by
## Chuck Smith

THE WORD
FOR TODAY

P.O. Box 8000, Costa Mesa, CA 92628 • Web Site: www.twft.com • E-mail: info@twft.com

Prayer Our Glorious Privilege
By Chuck Smith

© 2007, The Word For Today
Published by The Word For Today
P.O. Box 8000, Costa Mesa, CA 92628
(800) 272-WORD (9673)
Web Site: www.twft.com
E-mail: info@twft.com

ISBN: 978-1-597510-27-1

Fourth Printing, 2017

Editor: Shannon Woodward
Internal layout: Bob Bubnis

Printed in the United States of America.

# Contents

# FOREWORD

On a long-ago Saturday night, I sat in the second row of a church filled with 350 men and waited for the Calvary Chapel men's prayer meeting to begin. The seats around me filled quickly; those who arrived late took spots on the floor or stood against the wall. I was twenty-six years old, mentally damaged due to an overdose of drugs and too much alcohol usage, but newly saved—and loving the second chance at life God had given me.

While waiting, I struck up a conversation with a man who was twenty years old sitting in the row ahead of me. He told me that all his life, he had had epileptic fits and if he didn't take his daily medicine, his right side would go into convulsions. Understandably, the man was tired of the seizures and even more tired of the medication. He said he believed that God would heal him in the name of Jesus. As he rose to enter the line of people waiting for

Pastor Chuck Smith and the elders of the church to pray for and lay hands on them, I was struck by this young man's faith.

The Bible has this to say about faith: "Is anyone among you sick? Let him call for the elders of the church, and let them pray over him, anointing him with oil in the name of the Lord. And the prayer of faith will save the sick, and the Lord will raise him up. And if he has committed sins, he will be forgiven" (James 5:14-15).

As I had seen every Saturday night for as long as I had been attending Calvary Chapel Costa Mesa, the spiritual leaders of the church were fulfilling this verse. They were praying for the sick—and praying effectively.

While watching the epileptic man inch his way through the line, I remembered a verse from the gospel of Matthew, which I had only recently been taught. "Then behold, they brought to Him a paralytic lying on a bed. When Jesus saw their faith, He said to the paralytic, 'Son, be of good cheer; your sins are forgiven you'" (Matthew 9:2).

I watched that verse come to life on that long-ago Saturday night. The faith of the young man combined dynamically with the pastoral trust in prayer—and he was healed. Seeing the example of a faithful prayer—both on the part of the epileptic man and of the pastoral staff—I realized that I, too, could be healed. I believed that God wanted to heal me of the damage drugs had caused my mind. I went forward and presented myself to Pastor Chuck and the elders of the church. They laid their hands upon me, anointed me with oil, and prayed over me. And after two years of mental pain and anguish, that prayer of faith to God did for me what no doctor or medicine could do. In an instant of time, God in heaven took pity on me and restored my mind.

Pastor Chuck is a man who shows by his fruit that an effective prayer life is within the grasp of us all. As you read this book, be assured that these aren't just words from an author—this is a heavenly-inspired invitation. It is an easy-to-use, simple-to-read manual on the potential—and importance—of you and God working together to bring about a glorious prayer life.

May the Holy Spirit empower you to become a person of faith and prayer. May Jesus become real to you in a way that you have never before imagined. And may you go forth shining in faith, testifying, like the man who walked forward that Saturday night, of the God who is real.

Pastor Mike MacIntosh
Horizon Christian Fellowship
San Diego, CA
Author of *Falling in Love with Prayer*

# The Power of Prayer

The man was a Missouri state senator, a brilliant attorney—and an avowed atheist. His beautiful wife was a godly woman and a devoted Christian. Not surprisingly, their relationship suffered from this great spiritual divide. So she decided to do something about it.

One Tuesday, when this woman gathered with three of her friends for their weekly prayer meeting, she requested the others to make a covenant with her to pray for her husband's salvation. Every morning at ten o'clock, each would pray for her husband, asking, "God, please take hold of his heart and turn him toward Jesus Christ." Each agreed, and prayed faithfully for the senator from that morning on.

The woman's husband left for Congress knowing he was facing a particularly heavy session. Many important issues would come before the Senate during that session, several of which he had authored himself. When the first day of the new session ended, he felt tired, but as he explained later, he also felt something odd. He couldn't put his finger on what had changed, but he felt like something unusual was happening. Something was different.

That "something" made a difference. That particular session was so hectic; the senator barely had time to call home. But when he returned home during the congressional recess, he surprised his wife by suggesting—for the first time ever— that they go to church together. His wife, of course, was delighted. But the greatest surprise of all was yet to come. When the invitation was given at church that Sunday morning, the woman saw her prayers realized. Her husband went forward to receive Christ as his Lord and Savior.

Life changed dramatically after that. Though married many years, the couple found a new beginning as one in Christ. Thrilled at what God had done, the woman shared with her husband the covenant she had made with her friends to pray each morning for his salvation.

"When did you start doing that?" he asked.

"Well, let me see," she said, thinking. "I know it was on a Tuesday, because that is the day we meet for prayer." Checking the calendar, she found the date. "Here it is," she said. "This was when we started praying for you."

Her husband looked at the date and then, his eyes gleaming with excitement, said, "Let me show you something." He opened his diary to the same date and pointed to a notation at eleven o'clock in the morning— exactly ten a.m. in Missouri—where he had written, "I have suddenly come to a tremendous consciousness and awareness of my need for God. I don't understand what this is all about."

Oh, the power of prayer! And this story is just one of millions that demonstrate the mighty things that have been done through that one simple act.

And yet, we sometimes speak of prayer as though it is the least of our options, the weakest of our tools. How many times, when a need presents itself, have you heard yourself or others say, "Well, I guess all we can do is pray." *All* we can do?! The truth is, prayer is the most powerful weapon we possess, and the most important activity a Christian can perform.

Rather than the last desperate attempt we make after all our resources are depleted, prayer should be our first recourse. Prayer should head our list of priorities, for certainly the world around us is in desperate need of our prayers.

Prayer opens the door for God to do a glorious work in your life and in the lives of those around you. But too many of us have an ineffective or non-existent prayer life. That can change. That *must* change. This collection of studies on prayer presents you with Scriptures, thoughts, and principles on which to build an effective prayer life. When you put them into practice in your life, you will find, just as that Missouri senator did, that they will change your life. A dynamic prayer life softens hearts, moves mountains, and brings you into an entirely new and deepened relationship with God.

*Prayer Our Glorious Privilege* is categorized into three sections:

## PURPOSE

Here I explain the "what" of prayer. What is prayer, and what is its intent?

## PLAN

This section deals with the "how" of prayer. I will give you general principles and examples of how to pray, and how to make prayer effective in your own life.

## PROMISE

Finally, we will examine the "why" of prayer. I will share with you the powerful results and blessings of a life of prayer.

It is easy to read a book on prayer and walk away unchanged. Don't let that happen. Don't just read about prayer—practice it. Start praying right now, and pray daily.

Recognize that prayer is the most potent weapon in your spiritual arsenal, and use it with great promise and much hope—for when you begin a life of prayer, you begin a great adventure.

# THE PURPOSE

CHAPTER 1

# What is Prayer?

People often misunderstand the purpose of prayer. They think—mistakenly—that prayer is a way for us to get God to do the things we want done, and bring the things we desire. But that was never God's intention for prayer. The purpose of prayer is that we may join hands with God to accomplish *His* purposes here on earth, and to accomplish what otherwise might not have been done had we not prayed.

## EXPRESSIONS OF PRAYER

What does prayer look like? Our prayers can be expressed in three basic forms:

1. Worship
2. Petition
3. Intercession

Each form has variations, but these are the three primary types of prayer we offer to God. To help us better understand these expressions of prayer, let us look at their chief characteristics.

## PRAYER WORSHIPS GOD

The first basic form of prayer is worship. As we realize the greatness of God, His nearness to us, and His love for us, we can't help but respond to Him through the expression of deep, inner worship. The conscious awareness of God results naturally in the spontaneous act of worship.

I remember one day when I noticed a little gnat flying around me and found myself focusing on it. As I watched that tiny gnat—amazingly small, yet so wonderfully designed—I became captivated by what God had created. That gnat defied the laws of gravity, suspending itself in the air one second, then darting about the next. I thought, *"God, You are so wise in the way You have designed even the smallest forms of life."* In that moment, through my awareness of the magnificence of His creation, I was worshiping God.

Creation is a powerful motivator to worship. When we take the time to really see creation and remember its Creator, our consciousness of who He is and what He has done inspires us to worship. When I recognize the wisdom and power and goodness of God, I stand in awe of Him. In this way, worshiping God for His creative genius is a form of prayer.

I believe Christians should engage in this type of communion with God regularly, even constantly. We should take note of creation, for God reveals Himself through it. Through nature, we see God's power in a lightning storm, we smell His loveliness in a rose, we see His artful design in a daisy. As the old hymn reminds us, "In the rustling grass I hear Him pass; He speaks to me everywhere."[1] Worshiping God through prayer should become as natural to us as breathing in and out.

We often think of worship as being a verbal expression, but even when we don't speak a word, praise to God in the quiet of our hearts is still worship. Any time God manifests Himself to us—and He does so in a thousand different ways every day—and we feel overwhelmed and awed by Him, that is worship. We might lift our hands and exclaim, "Oh, God is so good!" Or we might say nothing at all, as we quietly commune with Him in the recognition of His love and grace. Whenever we recognize His greatness or acknowledge His position and power, we are worshiping God.

## PRAYER PETITIONS GOD

Whenever we bring our personal needs before God, asking Him for help, we engage in the prayer of petition.

---

[1] *This is my Father's World,* Maltbie D. Babcock, copyright 1901.

Some people dismiss personal petition prayer as selfish. They say you ought to ignore your own needs and concentrate on the needs of others. They say it is wrong to pray for yourself. But all you have to do is look in Scripture and you will find that is not true. David asked for protection and vindication. Solomon asked for wisdom. Even Jesus prayed for Himself on the cross, when He said, "Father, into Your hands I commit My spirit" (Luke 23:46). Those examples tell me it is not wrong to petition God for my own needs. Day by day I cry out to the Lord for His wisdom, guidance, strength, and provision.

Back in junior high school, as part of my initiation into the Hi Y Club, I had to memorize this poem by an unknown author:

> Lord, help me live from day to day,
> In such a self-forgetting way,
> That even when I kneel to pray,
> My prayer will be for others.
> Help me in all the work I do,
> To ever be sincere and true,
> And know that all I do for You,
> Must needs be done for others.
> Others, Lord, yes, others,
> Let this my motto be.
> Help me to live for others,
> That I might live for Thee.

This is beautiful poetry and it expresses an important truth. I *should* pray for others and be concerned with their needs.

But God wants me to know that I must also be concerned in prayer with my own needs. Before I can be of benefit to others, I have certain needs that must be met—and so do you. So petitioning God for our own needs is something He wants us to do regularly.

## PRAYER INTERCEDES WITH GOD FOR OTHERS

The third form of prayer is intercession, and this is the type of prayer that can be considered work. Worshiping God is not work—that is glorious! Worshiping God is spontaneous. It brings us into beautiful communion and fellowship with God. And I am not working hard when I petition God, because I am obviously interested in what I need. So it is easy to become involved in prayers of petition. But when I begin to intercede for others, then I find I must labor.

Paul supports this fact in his closing remarks to the church at Colosse, when he mentions one of his fellow laborers. "Epaphras, who is one of you, a bondservant of Christ, greets you, always laboring fervently for you in prayers, that you may stand perfect and complete in all the will of God" (Colossians 4:12). By using the phrase "laboring fervently," Paul is letting us know that this type of prayer is work.

Through intercessory prayer I reach out beyond myself. I am no longer praying for my own needs, but for the needs of those around me. I pray for my family, for my friends, and for my neighbors who don't yet know Jesus Christ. I pray for our nation and its leaders. I pray for the persecuted church around the world, and for the needs of other members in the body of Christ. When I intercede in prayer, I bring before God all the various needs of others that have come to my attention. It is amazing that we can enter into this kind of work, and it is amazing what can be accomplished through intercessory prayer.

In her later years, when she was in her mid 80s, it was my privilege to become Corrie ten Boom's pastor. At first, whenever she was in town she would come to our church in Costa Mesa. But after her stroke, when she was no longer able to attend church, she listened to our services on the radio.

Every once in awhile, Corrie's caretaker would call me from her home in nearby Placentia, and ask me to come visit her. One day I found her quite discouraged because of her physical impairment. She had always been such a vital, involved person. She had spent over thirty years traveling the world ministering and sharing her experiences. But now she couldn't leave her home, and it discouraged her greatly. She could not understand why God let her remain alive when she could no longer be active.

As I talked to her, God reminded me of a story I had heard about a woman in England whose prayer for revival brought a miraculous answer from God. So I shared the following story with Corrie:

At the end of a Saturday evening service in London, during which testimonies were shared in an open meeting, Dwight Moody testified of what God was doing in America and in his own ministry. When the meeting concluded, a pastor approached Moody and asked if he would preach at the pastor's church the following morning and evening. Dwight Moody consented, and the next morning went to the church to preach. He later said that once he began preaching, he wished fervently that he had not consented. He said he had never spoken to a colder, more unresponsive group of people in all his life. The experience was simply miserable—nothing but push, push, push, all the way. He even told some of his best jokes, but he couldn't get so much as a smile out of the crowd.

I have to interject here that I have felt that same particular misery before. Years ago, while visiting Korea and teaching through an interpreter in the largest Presbyterian church in the world, I told my best joke. I mean, it was my very best, sure-fire, no-fail joke. And I hit the punch line expecting at least a ripple of laughter—but I got nothing. The entire congregation just sat staring at me. Man, that was devastating. To comfort myself, I thought, "Well, evidently these people just aren't into humor."

When it was over, I asked my interpreter about the joke and discovered that he hadn't caught the punch line. He had completely mistranslated my joke. But what can you do? I learned after that to check out my jokes with the interpreters first. If they laughed, I would tell it. If they said, "But why did so-and-so do that?" I would say, "Let's skip that joke."

It is one thing when you lose a joke in translation. It is another when you are sharing that joke in your native language and it still falls flat. The congregation understood Moody. They just didn't respond. And Moody found himself getting angry that he had promised to come back that night. But he had given his word, and he had no choice but to return that evening. But oh, how he dreaded the thought. And sure enough, just as had been the case with the morning congregation, the evening crowd was equally cold and unresponsive—until, midway through his sermon, there was a noticeable change. A warmth came over the people, and not only did they begin listening to Moody, they began to respond. When he asked who would like to receive Jesus Christ, hands went up all over the auditorium. So many people raised their hands that Moody questioned whether or not they had really understood him. *"It must be a cultural difference,"* he thought. *"They don't realize that I am asking them to be born again."* So he carefully explained again that he was asking them to repent from their sins, commit themselves to Jesus Christ, and invite Him to take control of their lives. "All you who would like to receive Jesus, stand to your feet now." And they stood—whole rows of people.

The room was filled with standing people. Turning to the pastor, Moody asked, "What does this mean?"

"I'm sure I don't know," the pastor responded, "but keep going."

*"These British people just do not understand me,"* Moody thought. And so he explained it once more, point-by-point. "You who would like to receive Jesus Christ as your personal Savior and begin walking with Him, and experience the changed life He will bring, please meet me downstairs in the inquiry room."

Moody went downstairs to the inquiry room, and the people followed him. In fact, they packed the room.

The next morning, Moody headed for Scotland. But no sooner did he arrive at his hotel than he found a message waiting for him. "Please return to London. The people are hungry for a revival." So Moody returned and preached another two weeks. During that time, over 400 decisions were made for Jesus Christ in that formerly cold, unresponsive church in England.

Moody was no fool. He knew that it wasn't his preaching that had so changed the atmosphere in that church. He knew there had to be a reason for the move of God in the hearts of those people. So he determined to find that reason. He began making inquiries, one leading to another, until finally he was led upstairs to the bedroom of an elderly spinster who, years earlier, had been told by doctors she would never walk again. Hearing that she would spend the rest of her days in bed devastated the woman. "Oh God," she prayed, "I have always planned to serve You. But I have procrastinated, and now here I am, Lord. I'm so sorry I have wasted my life. Please forgive me. What a tragedy, Lord. I would so love to serve You, but now I can't do anything."

But the Lord spoke to the woman's heart, "You can pray." And so the bedridden woman began a ministry of intercessory prayer, and she concentrated especially upon the church she had attended there in London because it was so cold and formal. "Lord," she would pray, "please stir the church. Send a revival."

This woman had a sister who used to bring her meals every day. Sometimes she would bring up a newspaper or magazine, and one day, when she set a magazine down on the woman's bed, she picked it up and began reading an article about a young American minister named D. L. Moody. The article touched her heart and she felt moved to pray, "Lord, please send this young man to our church here in London and bring a revival to these people."

Day after day this woman prayed that same prayer. Each Sunday, when her sister would return home from church, this prayer warrior would ask, "How were the services today?" Almost without fail, her sister would reply, "The same as usual—same cold prayers, same cold songs, everything the same." But one Sunday, when her sister returned home from church and was asked that question, she answered, "We had a visitor today—a young minister from America."

At that, the bedridden woman perked up. "What was his name?"

Her sister paused. "Something kind of funny—Moody, I think."

The woman's heart skipped. "D. L. Moody?" she prompted.

"Yes! That's it."

The woman turned white. "Don't bring me any lunch today and don't allow any visitors to come upstairs," she instructed. "I've got business to do."

For the rest of that day, this woman bombarded heaven, asking God to break through the hearts of the people in that cold, unresponsive church. And He did.

After learning of these details, Moody later said, "I know that when we stand before Jesus to receive rewards for the things we have done, I will not receive any reward for the great move of God in those hundreds of souls who received Jesus Christ. The one who will receive that reward is the little woman who prayed faithfully for revival."

When I finished telling that story, I said, "Corrie, it just may be that God has yet to fulfill His greatest ministry through your life. After all, the final chapter isn't written yet. It could be more glorious than all of the other chapters so far. For it could be that God has called you to intercessory prayer. It is possible that right here from your bed, you could touch the world for Jesus Christ."

A twinkle came into her eyes and a smile grew on her face. We held hands and in her sweet Dutch accent she said, "Yea, yea." God had spoken to her heart about the amazing plans He still had for her. From that day, Corrie ten Boom began a ministry of intercessory prayer that touched the world—right from the bed where she lay, unable to get around. And only heaven can tell how many lives were affected by Corrie from her bedroom in Placentia.

It is never too late to intercede on behalf of others in prayer—and only God knows what those prayers can accomplish. If Corrie ten Boom could do it in her diminished state, any one of us can wield this power in partnership with God.

Prayer, then, is worship, petition, and intercession—but it is something more as well. Prayer is a conduit through which God gives us strength and wisdom.

## ASK AND RECEIVE

Jesus said, "Without Me you can do nothing" (John 15:5). This, of course, is true. However, we don't always live as though we believe Him. Sometimes in our stubbornness, we insist that there must be something good we can do apart from Jesus. We are always looking for some redeeming quality within ourselves, some characteristic for which God might love us. It would seem that we are incurably self-righteous.

"That's all right, Lord," we say. "I'll do this one. You don't have to help me this time." Then, when we fail, Jesus reminds us, "Without Me you can do nothing." I have proven the truth of that statement over and over in my own life. Apart from Christ I am weak and helpless.

On the other hand, I have discovered the beautiful truth of Philippians 4:13: "I can do all things through Christ who strengthens me." Through Christ I have strength to meet any situation and overcome any difficulty. In myself I am weak, but in Him I am strong.

Some people are naturally strong within themselves. They trust their own abilities and gloat in their independence and strength. However, no matter how strong a person thinks he is, the day will come when he exhausts his own resources. He will confess, "I can't do it! I can't go on!" For the man who has learned to trust only in himself, that is a tragic and disastrous day. But for the man who has learned to trust in the Lord, that day is no different than any other, because he has learned to turn every day over to God. The man who is self-reliant, self-willed, and self-made will ultimately fail. But the man who trusts in the Lord for his strength will never fail. As long as I look to myself and my own resources, I will always be restricted by my human limitations. But when I trust in God and in His resources, then I have His infinite capacities available to me.

I can never face a situation too big for God and me to handle. There is no obstacle so great that God and I can't overcome it together. There is no enemy too strong for God and me to defeat. God and I make a majority in any crowd! "If God be for me, who can be against me?" (Romans 8:31). God is our source of strength. And prayer is the channel through which God gives His strength.

Just as God is our strength, He is also our wisdom. As Scripture tells us, "The fear of the LORD is the beginning of knowledge, but fools despise wisdom and instruction" (Proverbs 1:7). When we fail to turn to God for the wisdom we need to live our lives, we prove ourselves to be fools.

Many times I have thought I could figure out the direction of my life without first consulting God—and many times I have been wrong. James tells us, "If any of you lacks wisdom, let him ask of God, who gives to all liberally and without reproach, and it will be given to him" (James 1:5). God is generous with His wisdom. All we have to do is ask. When we get to the point where we realize how hopelessly lost we are and we turn and ask Him for help, He is right there to meet us and set our feet on His path.

"For the LORD gives wisdom," the author of Proverbs tells us, "from His mouth come knowledge and understanding" (Proverbs 2:6). God is ready to give you wisdom; all you need to do is ask through prayer.

## A RIGHT PERSPECTIVE

If we are to have a right perspective of God's power, we must first realize the extent of God's wisdom.

God knows *everything* about your life. He knows the troubles you are going through and the situations you are facing. In fact, thousands of years ago, before the foundation of the world, God knew the specific problems you would be facing today. "Your eyes saw my substance, being yet unformed. And in Your book they all were written, the days fashioned for me, when as yet there were none of them" (Psalm 139:16). God saw every moment of every day of your life before you even drew a single breath. He saw it all—the joys, the sorrows, the challenges.

Not only did God know the problems you would face in this life, He also knew the answers He would work out for you. God isn't taken by surprise. He isn't at a loss for a solution to your problems. God has your whole situation totally under His control.

Even our enemy is subject to God's control. God knows exactly where Satan wants to tempt you and God is the One who gives him permission. Satan's actions do not diminish God's control, for Satan can do no more than what God allows him to do. God sets the boundaries for the enemy and says, "You can move in this box, but you can't go outside of it." All things are moving within the prescribed limits set by God.

Russia was once one of the most powerful military forces in the world. Not that long ago, she possessed armaments and megaton bombs and a tremendously powerful delivery system of ICBM's. When the Russians threatened, not many years ago, to bury us, the fact was they couldn't even have lifted a bomb off the ground unless God had allowed it. All things happen according to God's predetermined counsel. When you pray, remember that *nothing* is out of God's hand. God has everything under His control, and I might add, His timing is perfect—though it is often not in sync with ours.

Once you have God's perspective on your life and you realize to whom you are praying—how great God is, how wise He is, and how completely sovereign and powerful He is—your requests won't seem so impossible.

The Bible tells us that God created the heavens, the earth, the sea, and everything in them. David looked up at the night sky and said, "When I consider Your heavens, the work of Your fingers, the moon and the stars, which You have ordained, what is man that You are mindful of him?" (Psalm 8:3-4). Like David, it is good for us to look up once in awhile and remember God's creative power. It reassures us that God has all things under control. Thousands of years ago, He wrote about today's world condition. He predicted the events we are experiencing right now—it is all happening right on target, just as He said. Remember that. If God created the universe and controls all things within it, it's not hard for Him to take care of even the smallest annoyance in your life. So go ahead—ask Him to take away the pain of your toothache.

The greater our concept of God, the smaller our problems seem. However, most of the time when we pray we get right into the problem. "Oh, God! This is so big! This is so horrible!" We panic because the mountain seems impossibly high. But God created Mount Everest, and He could move it to another part of the universe if He so desired. There is no mountain too high for God. Jesus said, "If you have faith as a mustard seed, you will say to this mountain, 'Move from here to there,' and it will move; and nothing will be impossible for you" (Matthew 17:20).

How big is that mountain in front of you? "I don't know how I'm going to pay my bills next week!" you cry. "Where will I ever get the money?" Where do you think all the gold in the world came from? God created it. It's nothing for God to meet your needs. If you can realize His power, His wisdom, His sovereignty, then you can bring your request to God with confidence and ease.

In the Old Testament, King Asa said, "LORD, it is nothing for You to help, whether with many or with those who have no power" (2 Chronicles 14:11). In other words, it really makes no difference to God whether you have a big army or a small platoon. God is still the commanding officer, and the victory—or defeat—is completely in His hands.

In 1 Samuel chapter 14, Jonathan, Saul's son, arose and saw Israel's perennial enemy, the Philistines, camped in the distance. They had come with innumerable troops, clearly intending to wipe out the nation of Israel. Most of Saul's army had already deserted and fled across the Jordan River. The few troops left were hiding in caves. Looking around, he saw that the men were fast asleep. So he nudged his armorbearer. "Wake up!" Jonathan said. "Look at all those Philistines over there. I wonder if God wants to deliver the Philistines to Israel today. If He does, He doesn't need the whole army. He can deliver the enemy to the two of us just as easily as to the whole army. Let's venture over to the Philistine camp and see if God wants to do a work for us."

I love that! I love the faith and courage Jonathan displayed. He was really saying, "God doesn't need an army. He can work through the two of us as easily as an army."

So Jonathan and his armorbearer went into the camp of the Philistines and began attacking them. These two fellows alone started what turned out to be the routing of the whole Philistine army! (1 Samuel 14:1-18). It makes no difference to God whether you are weak or strong, whether you have a huge army, or whether you are all alone. When God is the captain of your army—or the captain of your life—victory is certain.

Gideon learned this same lesson. In Judges chapter 6, we are told that the Midianites had covered the land like grasshoppers. When the children of Israel would harvest their crops, those Midianites would move in and rip them off. It was a desperate situation for Israel. So the Lord called Gideon to gather some troops together and go against this huge army that had invaded the land. Gideon sounded the trumpet, and 32,000 men responded.

But the Lord said to Gideon, "This is a problem, Gideon. You've got too many men." I am sure Gideon thought, *"Lord, am I hearing You right? Did You really say that I have too many? Lord! I've only got 32,000 men! The enemy has over 130,000!"*

The Lord said, "I know the hearts of these people. If I deliver the Midianites into the hands of the 32,000, they will go around boasting and bragging about how tough they are. So go out and tell the fellows, 'All of you who are fearful, you're dismissed. You can go home.'"

So Gideon did so. And to his dismay, 22,000 men went home, leaving him with only 10,000. Gideon and his army were now outnumbered over thirteen to one!

Then the Lord said, "Gideon, this is a problem. You've still got too many men."

I imagine Gideon objected. But again, God explained what He was thinking. "I know the heart of these people. If I deliver the Midianites to the 10,000, they will boast and brag about how tough they were and how they whipped the enemy. I want you to take them down to the brook and let them get a drink of water, and watch them carefully. Those who cup the water in their hands and lap it like a dog, set them apart. Send home the others—the ones who put their faces in the water."

Gideon watched as 9,700 men put their faces down in the water and he had to send them home. And then God said, "I will deliver the Midianites unto these 300."

God knew what He was going to do. But He wanted the glory for the work.

God will frequently allow us to get into situations such as the one Gideon found himself in. Perhaps you will never face an army intent on destroying you. But you will face your own overwhelming situations. And it is when you get to that place of helplessness, that place where logic makes you throw your hands in the air and cry out in despair, "I can't do it! There is no way out!" that you have come to the best place of all. When you come to the end of yourself, victory is just around the corner—because you are finally ready to hand your problem to God. That is when He shows up and works on your behalf. He fights that battle for you. He conquers the enemy. And because the situation was clearly so impossible, God gets all the glory for its outcome. It is impossible to boast, because you had no hand in the victory. All you can do is praise God from whom all blessings flow.

If you want your faith to grow—and fuel your prayers—you need to gain the right perspective about God. Remember the wise words of King Asa. Remember what the Lord did for Jonathan, and for Gideon. Take a cue from David, and look up at the heavens. See God for who He is and recognize His power. When you do that, your prayer life will change dramatically. You will find yourself praying boldly and with confidence, because you know the mighty God who hears you is able to move on your behalf.

CHAPTER 2

# THE LISTENING SIDE OF PRAYER

We have all known people who dominate a discussion. You ask them one simple question and it's like you have wound them up. They start talking and they just don't stop. As they are talking, you think of something you would like to say, but they won't stop long enough to give you a chance. And by the time they do decide to take a breath, you have already forgotten what you wanted to say. That is not a dialogue—that is a monologue.

Prayer is supposed to be a two-way conversation with God. But as we have already discussed, this isn't always the case. All too often, like those people we know who like to dominate the conversation, we do the same thing to God. We hog the conversation.

## A TWO-WAY CONVERSATION

Our prayer needs to be a two-way conversation with God, not a one-sided speech. This, too, speaks of a need for a right perspective. If I am convinced that what God has to say to me is much more important than what I have to say to God, I will listen!

The listening side of prayer is critical. We must learn to recognize God's voice—and then we must learn to listen. When we do so, we discover those things God wants to do in and through our lives. It helps us to learn what we should be asking God in our prayers. And when we know we are praying according to God's will, we pray with great confidence. We come to trust the words of John, who said, "If we ask anything according to His will, He hears us. And if we know that He hears us, whatever we ask, we know that we have the petitions that we have asked of Him" (1 John 5:14-15).

And that brings us back to our initial definition of prayer: It is a means by which God accomplishes His will on the earth. It is all about His will, not our own. It is a fact that bears repeating: prayer is not a marvelous mechanism designed by God for getting our wishes and our will done here on earth. This is how many of us view prayer. We think of prayer as a way to get a bigger home, or a better car, or some promotion we want on the job. We are quick to tell God what we want Him to do for us, but we are not always quick to consider what He might want us to do for Him, or what He wants to accomplish through us. That understanding comes only when we attend to the listening side of prayer.

As I think back on my life—especially during my early years of walking with the Lord—and remember the things I tended to pray for at that time, I am so glad God didn't say yes more often. I will admit that I was sometimes upset with God over those denials. In the back of my mind, I thought that if He loved me, He would do those things I asked Him to do. But I wasn't always praying for God's will back then. More often, I prayed for my own will.

This is why it is so important to understand and practice the listening side of prayer. Let God speak to you; let Him direct the conversation and steer your heart in the direction of His will, and then make that your prayer.

You see, true prayer really begins with God. It starts in the heart of God, with the purposes of God, in the things that God wants to do. He then plants those ideas and longings in *your* heart. He speaks to you. If you listen, He will reveal His purpose and His plan to you. Then you, in turn, offer those things up in prayer to Him. This is a wonderful, God-designed cycle, beginning with the heart of God, coming down through your heart, passing back to God in prayer, and then opening the door and the opportunity for God to do the things He desires to do.

God could override your will if He chose to do so. But He doesn't. Instead, He works in your heart and draws you to Himself, speaking to you, revealing His wisdom to you, until you get to the point where you surrender your will to Him. Only then—only when you have yielded your own desires and have begun to pray about His desires—will God begin to work out His will in your life. If we don't align ourselves with His will, then we are the ones who miss out. And the way to align our will with His is to pray. It is a beautiful partnership that begins when we dialogue with God.

## ELIJAH: A MAN OF LIKE PASSIONS

In a quest to build a powerful, effective prayer life, it is helpful and even wise to look at examples of people who demonstrated that kind of prayer life. Later we will look at more examples, but for the purposes of this discussion, we want to take a moment to look at Elijah. Here was a true prayer warrior, and a man who understood the listening side of prayer.

In 1 Kings, we read that Elijah called down fire from heaven, raised the son of a widow woman from the dead, and worked a variety of miracles. James tells us that when Elijah prayed for the rain to stop, it didn't rain for three-and-a-half years. Then he prayed for it to rain—and it did!

It is hard to identify with Elijah. His exploits were so amazing, we think of him as someone out of reach for ordinary people. He seems way beyond the average God-follower. But James 5:17 tells us that "Elijah was a man with a nature like ours." In other words, he was just like you and me—a man of like passions. Elijah knew what it was to be afraid. He knew what it was to be discouraged. He knew all the emotions and weaknesses that we experience. So when we read that God used him mightily, in spite of his human frailties, we realize that God can use us, too.

Elijah can teach us much concerning prayer. His story confirms that prayer is not, and should never be, a monologue. Rather, prayer is truly a dialogue—it is a conversation with God.

In 1 Kings 17:1, Elijah came to King Ahab and said, "As the LORD God of Israel lives, before whom I stand, there shall not be dew nor rain these years, except at my word." What Elijah was saying was, "I am going to pray and God is going to shut up heaven. This will go on for many years, for you will not have rain again until I say so, or until I pray and ask God to bring it."

After this, the Lord told Elijah to go into hiding. And there came a horrible drought in the land. Streams and rivers dried up, and the people became hungry and desperate. Enraged, King Ahab sent his men searching all over the land for Elijah. They scoured the countryside, even threatening people who might know where Elijah was hiding.

But then we read in 1 Kings 18:1, "And it came to pass after many days that the word of the LORD came to Elijah, in the third year, saying, "Go, present yourself to Ahab, and I will send rain on the earth."

God was telling Elijah that He was going to send rain upon the earth again. Elijah heard and understood because he was in the habit of listening for God, and he recognized His voice.

So Elijah let Ahab know he was ready to meet with him. Ahab came to him and said, "You are the man who has troubled Israel."

Then Elijah said, "No, I haven't troubled Israel. You have troubled Israel by teaching the people to worship the god *Baal*. But if you are up to it, I want to challenge you and your god to a contest. We'll gather on the top of Mount Carmel. You bring the prophets of *Baal* and I will meet you there. Your prophets can build an altar there to *Baal*, and I will build an altar to *Jehovah*. We'll both put wood and sacrifices on our altars. Then your prophets can pray to *Baal* to spontaneously kindle a fire to consume the sacrifice, and I will pray to *Jehovah* to send fire to consume the sacrifice. And the god that answers by fire, let Him be acknowledged as the true God."

So Ahab took up the challenge, and the people of Israel gathered at the top of Mount Carmel. The prophets of

Ahab built their altar and placed the wood and the sacrifice upon it. And in the morning they began to pray to *Baal* to send fire to consume the sacrifice. They screamed and danced, jumped up and down, and carried on.

By about noon, when fire had not appeared, Elijah decided to have a little fun with them. "I know what the problem is," he said. "Your god must be sleeping. You've got to cry louder. You've got to wake him up. Or maybe he has stepped away, and you need to yell so he'll hear you."

So now they really began to scream. They leaped up onto the altar. They cut themselves with knives, making a big bloody mess. But no matter what they tried, they couldn't get *Baal* to kindle a fire, and they couldn't get the heavens to pour forth rain.

About three o'clock in the afternoon, Elijah said, "Okay, you have had your chance. Now it is my turn. Stand back." Then, to further rub salt in their wounds, he said, "Dig a trench around my altar and pour water over the top of my sacrifice."

So they poured on the water—barrels and barrels of water.

Elijah shouted, "More! Pour more water!"

So they soaked the sacrifice until it was covered with water and even the trench around it was filled with water.

Then Elijah prayed. He didn't dance or shout or scream, he simply said, "LORD God of Abraham, Isaac, and Israel, let it be known this day that You are God in Israel and I am Your servant, and that I have done all these things at Your word."

The fire of God came down. It not only consumed the sacrifice, it consumed the water and licked up the water in the trenches. And there was a great, great moving of God's Spirit on the people. They fell on their faces crying, "The LORD, He is God! The LORD, He is God!"

Elijah took advantage of the opportunity. He ordered the people to take the priests and the prophets of *Baal* down to the Brook Kishon in the valley below. There, Elijah killed all 450 prophets of *Baal*.

Now with the prophets of *Baal* dead and gone, Elijah announced, "Get ready! There is going to be a downpour of rain!" Then he went back up to the top of the mountain with his servant, got on his face before the Lord, and began to pray for rain. He said to his servant, "Go out and look towards the sea." From the top of Mount Carmel, you get a great view of the Mediterranean Sea. But when the servant came back he said he had seen nothing but blue sky.

So Elijah prayed again and then he said to the servant, "Go and look out towards the sea." But again the servant reported, "Nothing but blue sky."

They repeated this scenario until by the seventh time, when Elijah told his servant to go and look toward the sea, the servant came back and said, "There is a little cloud rising out of the sea about the size of a man's fist."

"Get to the shelter," Elijah said. "There is going to be a downpour!" And before they could run for cover, the rain began falling.

How could Elijah have been so persistent in prayer, so sure God was up to something? After six times, when there was no evidence, no sign—how is it he kept on praying and giving his servant the same instructions?

The reason he could do it is because Elijah heard from the Lord. God had told him to present himself to Ahab because He was about to send rain upon the earth. When God tells you something, you can believe it. You can rely on it. Elijah was confident that God would do just as He had said. So his prayer—and the persistence behind it—was built upon the Word of God and the promises of God.

Elijah showed enormous faith in that situation. But not long after, he proved he was an ordinary man like you and me. When King Ahab's wife, Queen Jezebel, heard what Elijah had done to her prophets, she sent a messenger to him saying, "So let the gods do to me, and more also, if I do not make your life as the life of one of them by tomorrow about this time" (1 Kings 19:2).

When Elijah heard the threats of Jezebel, he became frightened and ran. Elijah ran! And not just a little way. He ran all the way down to Beersheba, about one hundred and twenty miles south. Then he went a day's journey beyond Beersheba, where he sat down under a juniper tree and cried out, "Lord, kill me! It's all over!" Elijah was tired, discouraged, and terrified.

Here is our great man of faith, Elijah, running for his life—a man of like passions, just like you and me.

This story inspires and encourages me. To see that even Elijah—who is one of my heroes—had the same weaknesses I do, reminds me that God uses plain, ordinary men and women.

You don't have to be some super saint! You don't need big credentials or a long list of awards and titles behind your name. God uses regular people—people who feel just like you feel. He uses people who know what it is like to be discouraged, just as you know what it is like to be discouraged. He uses people who know what it means to have fears, just like you have from time to time.

But Elijah was a man who listened for the voice of God, heard it, and responded. We can do that too. Remember, it is not the man; it is the God who speaks through the man. Any one of us can be an Elijah for our day—just listen, hear, and respond when God speaks to you.

God ministered to Elijah in his fear. The Lord sent an angel to bring food to Elijah. "Eat," the angel said. "You are going to need the strength." So Elijah ate—and journeyed forty days on the strength of that angel food. He traveled all the way to Mount Horeb, way down in the wilderness, and when he got there, God's great man of fear was still so terrified of Jezebel's threats that he hid in a cave.

Before long, God came to him in the cave and said, "Elijah, what are you doing here?" (1 Kings 19:9).

Cornered, Elijah explained himself to God—as if God didn't already know what he was up to. "Oh! I have been zealous for the LORD God of hosts," he said. "Israel has forsaken Your covenant. They have thrown down Your altars. They have killed Your prophets. I'm the only one left and now they are trying to kill me! God, I'm afraid You are about out of business. It is almost over."

God, of course, knew that the story was far from over. "Elijah," God said, "there is work to be done. Now get on up to Syria, anoint Hazael as king, give him a commission, and get back to work. You know you have no business hiding here." So the discouraged, terrified prophet was re-commissioned by God and he emerged from the cave.

Elijah was a man of like passions, but he was also a man who dialogued with God. Because of his example, we learn of the confidence we can have in prayer. Elijah shows us that when we know we are praying according to God's will and we listen for His voice, we will hear Him when He speaks to us, and we will see His desires revealed.

## LEARNING TO HEAR THE VOICE OF GOD

Elijah was able to act with confidence because he knew whose voice he was listening to. He knew that God had spoken to him. Like Elijah, we need to learn to tune in to God's voice. I am convinced that God is constantly speaking and that He speaks directly to each one of us. But we don't always recognize His voice. We dismiss what we hear as being our own thoughts. *"That is just something I'm thinking myself."* Oh, what we miss out on when we explain away God's voice!

In a world as busy and chaotic as this world is, it can be easy to miss God's voice. Our minds can be so cluttered with noise that His voice is drowned out. This is something we have to fight against. We have to train our minds to recognize His voice in the midst of the noise and confusion.

How can you train yourself to hear the voice of God? Well, first we need to recognize that God has *already* spoken to all of us. God has spoken to us through His Word. We can hear His voice through the words of the Bible.

In the book of Hebrews we read, "God, who at various times and in various ways spoke in time past to the fathers by the prophets, has in these last days spoken to us by His Son ..." (Hebrews 1:1-2).

The Bible declares that God *has* spoken to us! The Bible is God's Word to us. He *has* spoken and He *wants* to continue to speak to you through His Word.

How does He do that? One common experience is when you are reading a familiar passage of Scripture and you suddenly have a brand new insight. It might be a verse you have read dozens—or hundreds—of times before, but suddenly your eyes are opened to something you never saw before. Truth almost jumps off the page at you.

Train yourself to tune in to those moments. And realize that when those bits of insight and inspiration come to you, that is God speaking. The more time you spend reading God's Word and listening for His voice, the more often you will have those moments.

Recently, I had one of these glorious experiences as I was preparing a message. I happened to be in a passage I had studied many times before and knew well, but as I read, the Holy Spirit opened my eyes and began to speak to me through those verses. He gave me new insight and understanding. It is always beyond exciting when God speaks to you through His Word.

George Mueller was a man noted for his faith in the Lord. He spent years establishing orphanages in England, supported solely by his extraordinary faith. Many times in the morning there would be no food for breakfast, but he would lead the children in a prayer of thanksgiving for breakfast anyhow, knowing full well there was nothing in the kitchen.

Without fail, there would come a knock on the door and a fellow would say something like, "I have a dairy wagon out here pulled by horses, and the wheel is broken. I won't be able to make the route and the milk will sour. Maybe you can use it." He would bring the milk in and the children would have milk. And then someone else would come along with something else they needed.

Such was life for this man of faith. How did he know the Lord would provide? He just knew his Lord.

When you hear about a man like that, people often want to know what his devotional life was like. So they would ask George Mueller how many chapters of the Bible he read every day. And his answer surprised them. He said, "I only read until God speaks to me! When God speaks to me, then I just stop and meditate on that. Maybe while I'm reading the very first verse," he said, "that is when God decides to speak to me. And that is my verse for the day. Sometimes, I can read as much as ten chapters before the Lord speaks to me. But I read until He speaks to me."

That is a good practice! Why not be like George Mueller and just read until God speaks to you?

Open to Genesis and start reading through the Bible. Each morning, read until God speaks to you. When God does speak to you, underline that verse, or maybe write it out and carry it through the day. Meditate on it. Ruminate on it, like a cow chewing its cud. Think about the verse God gave you and ponder it until it feeds your heart and becomes a part of your life.

## THREE SIMPLE STEPS TO HEAR GOD'S VOICE

If we want to have a powerful, effective prayer life, it begins with hearing God's voice. We can learn to hear Him by applying these three simple steps:

## 1. READ EXPECTANTLY

When I sit down and engage in what I like to call a "wide reading of Scripture," I often keep a pen and ruler in my hand, because I expect God to speak to me through the Word. And because I am expecting Him to speak, He does. So if I have the pen and the ruler handy, I can underline how God spoke to me and what He said on that day and in that moment.

Before you read, find a quiet place where you are not apt to be interrupted. It is too easy to let yourself get distracted. You want to be sure to focus your attention on God. Then as you are reading, get in the habit of praying the promises you find in Scripture.

For instance, let's say you are reading in Proverbs and you come to chapter 3, verses 5 and 6. As you are reading along, pray those verses to God. "Lord, I want to trust You with my whole heart. Help me to put all my faith, all my trust in You. Keep me from making decisions without You. Don't let me rely on my own thoughts or my own understanding. Prompt me to acknowledge You in all my decisions, and to wait for Your input." Then when you read the promise in verse 6, you can pray that back to God as well. "Lord, I see that when I do that—when I acknowledge You in all my decisions—You promise that You will direct my path. I want that, Lord. I need Your guidance."

Your prayer life will be greatly enhanced when you base it on God's Word. Often God will use a specific verse to speak directly to a problem you are facing or an issue you have been praying about. All the answers you need are right there in His Word. Within those pages, God declares what He will do for you. He speaks His promises. Then, like Elijah, you stand on those promises.

One other word about this time of prayer and reading: I strongly suggest that before you pick up a commentary or some other resource, you read the Bible first. I am thankful for good commentaries and for the men who have written them. I am glad those scholars have recorded their thoughts and understanding of particular Scriptures—these tools are often very helpful. But before I read what God has said to other men, I want to give Him an opportunity to speak to my heart first. So it is only *after* I have studied a passage of Scripture and given God the opportunity to speak to me personally that I will then read the commentaries on that particular passage. After I have listened to what God has to say to me, I will find out what God has said to others.

## 2. READ PRAYERFULLY

The truths of God are not always revealed to the keen mind, but to the Spirit-filled mind.

People sometimes believe that the only way they can truly understand Scripture is to have knowledge of Greek and Hebrew, the original languages of the Bible. There is definite value in studying the Greek language and the

Hebrew language. I use A. T. Robertson's *Grammar of the Greek New Testament* and Joseph Thayer's *Greek-English Lexicon,* and other helpful study aids. It is certainly helpful to understand the background of the words and their original meanings. But we must be careful that along with those little bits of understanding we don't also pick up a little smugness. It is easy to begin thinking, "How wonderful that I have this knowledge of the Greek! Oh, these nuggets of truth I have discovered! It is too bad other people don't know the Greek language better."

The truth is, it's not as important to know what God said in another language long ago as it is to know what He is saying to your heart right now.

Years ago, there was a lady in my church who had never attended school beyond the sixth grade. But she would often come up to me on a Sunday morning and say, "Pastor Smith, I was reading in Galatians this week and I found something interesting … " and she would begin to explain something she had read that turned out to be the same nugget of truth I thought I had gotten just because I understood the Greek.

"Lord, that isn't fair!" I would think. "She didn't spend all those hours and all that misery trying to learn Greek. You just gave that insight to her!"

So you see, it isn't to the keen mind that God speaks—it is to the Spirit-filled mind. You don't have to know Hebrew. You don't have to know Greek. You don't have to know the grammars, the tenses, or the different nuances to a particular word. God can speak to you by His Spirit, giving you understanding and enlightenment of His Word and of His truth. Read prayerfully and allow His Spirit to reveal His truths to your heart.

## 3. READ THOUGHTFULLY

When you read Scripture, don't skim across it like it is a novel. These are the words of God—the very thoughts and expressions of the Creator of the universe. Take your time to absorb the truth of the Scriptures. Meditate on the verses you read. When you sense God speaking to you—respond. Do what He is telling you to do. Obedience greatly enhances your relationship with God! As you read, and He speaks, and you respond, your prayer life will come alive. No longer will it be just a one-sided conversation, but a living, active dialogue.

CHAPTER 3

# THE BATTLE

Prayer, as we have seen, is a means whereby God accomplishes His will on the earth. As we have discussed, prayer is a way to worship God, to intercede on behalf of others, to petition God for our needs, and to gain strength and wisdom. But there is another aspect of prayer that is vital to the life of the believer, and which requires more in-depth discussion. Prayer is a weapon. When we enter into intercessory prayer for others, we enter a battleground.

The world which we see with our eyes is not the only world that exists. Invisible to our physical eyes is the spirit world, which is divided into two categories: God's forces of good, and Satan's forces of evil. Between these two forces, a battle wages continually for the souls of men. The moment we begin to intercede for another person, we rush into the thick of the battle. In fact, we step right up to the frontlines of the battle. Spiritual warfare is fought on our knees.

This kind of prayer, the warfare praying in the Spirit, becomes real work because you are engaged against the forces of darkness and hell. You begin to understand what Paul meant when he said that Epaphras was laboring fervently in prayer. Through prayer, you can advance with the battering ram and demolish the strongholds the enemy has on individual lives—freeing them from the power by which the enemy holds them captive.

Since prayer draws you right into the heart of battle—a battle fought against evil spirits—you ought to prepare yourself first. No soldier ever enters the battlefield without first donning his armor.

## DRESSED FOR BATTLE

The apostle Paul said, "We do not wrestle against flesh and blood, but against principalities, against powers, against the rulers of the darkness of this age, against spiritual hosts of wickedness in the heavenly places" (Ephesians 6:12).

This is not like any battle on earth. This is a battle in the spirit world. And in order to be fit for this battle, Paul tells us we are to dress accordingly. "Therefore take up the whole armor of God, that you may be able to withstand in the evil day, and having done all, to stand. Stand therefore, having girded your waist with truth, having put on the breastplate of righteousness, and having shod your feet with the preparation of the gospel of peace; above all, taking the shield of faith with which you will be able to quench all the fiery darts of the wicked one. And take the helmet of salvation, and the sword of the Spirit, which is the word of God; praying always with all prayer and supplication in the Spirit, being watchful to this end with all perseverance and supplication for all the saints" (Ephesians 6:13-18).

Because we are not engaged in a physical battle, our armor can't be physical—it must be spiritual. And the same holds true of our weapons.

## THE WEAPONS

Christians sometimes have funny ideas about weaponry. We have been given so many powerful options—prayer, God's Word, fasting—and yet we sometimes choose to rely on lesser weapons to reach those around us. I think of the woman I heard about who used to put witnessing tracts in her husband's sandwiches, hoping that when he chomped down he would pull out this gooey little tract, smothered with peanut butter, and somehow "get" the truth. Others hope that by leaving Christian articles out on the table, a loved one will pick one up and read it, and somehow be converted that way. We devise all these little plans and methods, believing that we can do a spiritual work with physical methods. But "the weapons of our warfare are not carnal but they are mighty through God" (2 Corinthians 10:4).

## GOD'S WORD

One of the first weapons of our warfare is the Word of God itself. The Bible declares, "For the word of God is living and powerful, and sharper than any two-edged sword" (Hebrews 4:12). In speaking of our spiritual armament in Ephesians 6:17, Paul urges us to "take the sword of the Spirit, which is the Word of God." God's Word is a powerful weapon against the attacks of the enemy. Jesus used it every time Satan came at Him with temptation. "But He answered and said, 'It is written, Man shall not live by bread alone, but by every word that proceeds from the mouth of God'" (Matthew 4:4).

David understood the power of God's Word when he wrote, "Your Word I have hidden in my heart, that I might not sin against You" (Psalm 119:11). If you read it, meditate on it, and rely upon it, God's Word becomes a powerful weapon in your life against the temptations the enemy places before you. An old Swedish proverb says, "This Book will keep you from sin, and sin will keep you from this Book." Resist the distractions that rise up when you sit down to study God's Word. Make your reading of it a priority in your life. Memorize verses. Put the power of the Word of God to work in your life—keeping you from sin and delivering others from bondage.

## PRAYER

As we have been discussing throughout this book, prayer is a great weapon God has placed in our spiritual arsenal. More battles are won through prayer than by any other means. Knowing this, I find it strange that so often people use prayer only as a last resort. After they have tried everything they can think of and nothing has worked, they say, "I guess we had better pray. Things are really desperate."

Often people will come in for counsel and lay out their problem. "I did this and I tried that," they will say. Finally you ask, "Have you prayed about this yet?"

"Well, no," they answer, "I thought I would just come to you."

Why do we do this? God has given us this powerful weapon of prayer and we don't use it. It is fine to seek the help and counsel of trusted believers, but through prayer, we can receive our counsel directly from God Himself.

Prayer is an amazing weapon. And it is available to everyone. You don't have to be a spiritual giant to enter the battlefield—God has made prayer available to even the weakest of His children.

## FASTING

No discussion of spiritual weaponry would be complete without the mention of fasting. In Matthew chapter 17, a distraught father came to Jesus and knelt down before

Him. He then asked for mercy for his son—an epileptic who had suffered severely. When the man told Jesus that he had brought his son to the disciples, but they were unable to cure him, Jesus rebuked the demon, cured the child, and then instructed the disciples on the weaponry they needed for that kind of battle. He first pointed out that they had lacked the faith to do the work, and then He said, "However, this kind does not go out except by prayer and fasting" (Matthew 17:21).

Why is fasting so powerful? I believe the answer is two-fold. First, fasting weakens our flesh. This is always a good thing, for the flesh does nothing but war against our spirit. The flesh is prone to disbelief, especially when it observes the work of the enemy. That may have been why the disciples were helpless to cast the demon out of the epileptic boy—they were overcome with doubt.

Secondly, fasting strengthens our spirit. In the war between the flesh and the spirit, any time the flesh is weakened, the spirit is automatically strengthened. When doubt is removed, faith rises. As Jesus said in this passage in Matthew, "If you have faith as a mustard seed, you will say to this mountain, 'Move from here to there,' and it will move; and nothing will be impossible for you" (Matthew 17:20).

Is there someone in your life you are praying for who is in such darkness that the task seems impossible? Then you need the kind of faith that moves mountains. In that situation, fasting would build your faith and strengthen your prayers.

One other word about the weapons God has given us: It seems to me that as Christians, we spend too much time trying to defend our weapons instead of just using them. For instance, when people argue against the Bible, we begin to defend it. The Bible is a great weapon, a sharp two-edged sword. Don't defend it—use it! If you are in a duel, you don't say, "You had better watch out—this sword has the sharpest steel in town. It has been honed to a super-fine edge." You don't defend your sword. You use your sword!

Likewise, we are always talking about our weapon of prayer. Don't talk about prayer—pray. Use the weapons God has given you and triumph over the enemy!

It bears repeating, over and over: "The weapons of our warfare are mighty through God for pulling down strongholds." Oh, that we would remember that, and use these weapons God has made available to us! God has given us His armor for protection: His Word as our sword for both offensive and defensive battle; fasting, through which we deny our flesh and strengthen our spirit; and prayer, through which we can pull down the enemy's strongholds.

With this armor, we are fit for the battle.


## READY?

Once you are fully equipped and dressed in your spiritual armor, don't just stand there—get into the fight! But how? How do you attack an unseen enemy? You take on the enemy when you pray.

Prayer is our greatest weapon against Satan's forces of darkness, and the frontlines of this war is in the prayer closet. "Praying always with all prayer and supplication in the Spirit, being watchful to this end with all perseverance and supplication for all the saints" (Ephesians 6:18). Once you are girded for the battle—it is time to go to it!

## THE BATTLE

Though invisible to our human eyes, the spirit world is just as real as the material world. Within that spirit world, two opposing forces battle one another. One force is composed of angels who are obedient to God, who serve in His kingdom of life and light. On the other side are spirits who have rebelled against God, who serve Satan's kingdom of death and darkness. What's interesting is that although we can't see these opposing forces and don't even think about them often, the major battlefield of their conflict is here on planet earth. You and I are in the midst of this battle for the control of our very lives. As these spirit forces are at war over you, often you will find yourself in the midst of conflict.

These spirit forces battle for the souls of men in general, but they also wage war over each of us individually. The battle is constant. And the two who fight for us employ vastly different tactics.

Satan tries to win the world through deception and manipulation. In his efforts to pull us away from God, Satan will use force if necessary. Jesus Christ also has a method of winning the world, but not by force. Jesus seeks to draw men unto Himself and into His kingdom through love.

Satan tries to persuade us to give in to that natural characteristic of greed and live only for ourselves; God seeks to soften our hearts toward those around us so we can reach out in love and give a hand of strength and blessing to those who have fallen.

Satan's way is tempting. It is much easier to close off our hearts and minds to those in need around us, to just go for what we can get for ourselves and to live a completely self-centered life. Sometimes we are tempted to tell those in need, "I worked hard for what I've got! You go work hard for your own needs. What's mine is mine and I'm not willing to share it or give it away. If you want something, you go earn it."

But because I belong to God, His Spirit is constantly speaking to my heart, saying, "Don't you see how you have been blessed? You have enough. Share what you have! Look around and notice all the needs. Show a little compassion. Be like My Son."

The apostle Paul wrote in Galatians 5:17 that "the flesh lusts against the Spirit, and the Spirit against the flesh; and these are contrary to one another." And so the battle of the flesh against the Spirit and the Spirit against the flesh is unending. Satan applies tremendous force and pressure to keep people in his camp. Jesus, wooing and drawing through gentle love, seeks to persuade men to submit their lives to Him. As long as we are in these bodies of flesh, we will find ourselves in the midst of this battle. The whole issue of life is this: Who shall rule my life? Satan or Jesus? Greed or love?

As I am engaged in this battle, prayer is the deciding factor for delivering victory. Satan knows that, and that is why it is so hard to pray.

Have you noticed that whenever you get on your knees and begin to pray, the doorbell rings, your phone beeps, or something else interrupts you? If it seems there is an almost diabolical connection between that portion of the carpet where you kneel and the telephone—it's because there is. The phone is a distraction. The person at the door—for that moment, at least—is a distraction. Anything that would pull you away from prayer is a distraction. Satan will do absolutely anything to keep you from prayer, because he knows it has the power to defeat him. And so he concentrates his efforts on disarming you.

When you realize how powerful prayer is, you really can't blame Satan for trying to stop you from using that weapon. He is terrified of prayer because he knows it is the deciding factor in the battle. When you stop to pray, it is like you have drawn a huge sword and have begun swinging it. He has nothing at all with which to counter our blows. So he will stop at nothing to try to keep that sword out of our hands.

What is crazy is that Satan is fighting a losing battle—and he knows it.

## THE HISTORY OF THE WAR

It is not often that you can know the outcome of a war while the war is still being fought, but in this battle between Satan and God, we already know the decision. This war has been fought and won. Two thousand years ago, the major contestants met head on, and one of them carried away the victory trophy while the other slunk away in defeat. This battle was fought at the cross, and it was there Christ defeated the enemy. Yet even though Jesus thoroughly conquered the enemy, that stubborn loser refuses to relent or give up. Since that time, he has sought to hold by force that which is no longer rightfully his.

In Colossians 2:14-15, Paul tells us about this battle and about the victory Jesus wrought, "having wiped out the handwriting of requirements that was against us, which was contrary to us. And He has taken it out of the way, having nailed it to the cross. Having disarmed principalities and powers, He made a public spectacle of them, triumphing over them in it."

You see, the world originally belonged to God by right of divine creation. God formed the earth, created man, and placed him upon it. When He did so, He gave the earth to man that he might enjoy it. God said, "Be fruitful and multiply; fill the earth and subdue it; have dominion over the fish of the sea, over the birds of the air, and over every living thing that moves on the earth" (Genesis 1:28). "It is all yours," He said to them. "Enjoy it."

But Satan came into the garden, and using lies, deceit and guile, he deceived man into turning the world over to him so that the world came under Satan's dominion and authority. He became the prince of the world and the world became his kingdom. Today as you look at the world, you do not see the unmarred beauty God created in the garden of Eden, nor do you see the world as God intended it to be. God did not create man to live in greed, and fight, and be at war with one another. It was God's plan that man should live in love and in harmony and be at peace with one another. But the world rebelled against God, and remains now in defiance.

God sent His Son Jesus Christ to redeem the world back to Himself. Jesus said that He came "to seek and to save that which was lost" (Luke 19:10). The purpose of Christ's coming was to bring the world back under the authority of God—to establish it again as God's kingdom. Jesus talked frequently to His disciples about the kingdom of God and the glories we would all see when the kingdom of God should come, when God once again ruled over the earth. Satan was fully aware of why Jesus came, which is why the conflict between Satan and Jesus began early—

when Jesus was less than two years old—and why Satan continually sought to destroy Jesus.

Satan first attempted to obstruct God's plan by inspiring the heart of Herod to issue a heinous decree. Herod ordered the slaughter of all babies two years and under. Had the angel of the Lord not warned Joseph to take the baby and his mother and flee to Egypt, Jesus would have been destroyed before He ever had the chance to redeem the world.

Later, after Jesus was baptized by John, He went into the wilderness, where Satan came to tempt Him. He took Jesus into a high mountain and showed Him all of the kingdoms of the world and the glory of them. And Satan said, "All these things I will give You if You will fall down and worship me" (Matthew 4:9).

Satan offered Jesus a compromise—but it was a lie, all part of his deceitful plan. You see, if Jesus had bowed down to worship him, then Jesus would have been in subjection to him and the world would have remained in Satan's hands. It was all a clever ruse. So Satan lied and said, "Here is a compromise. I'll make You a deal. You don't have to take God's way. You don't have to walk God's path. I will give You what You are looking for immediately. You don't have to suffer the cross. You don't have to take that painful way. You can have immediate fulfillment now. Just bow down and worship me. Follow my way." He tried to tempt Jesus to turn aside from God's path to follow his.

Satan says the same thing to people today. "You don't want to deny yourself," he whispers whenever we are tempted. "You don't want to have to take up a cross! Why not just follow me and I will grant you the immediate fulfillment you're looking for? You can have all the pleasure and excitement you want. I'll give it to you, if you'll just follow me."

When that offer was made to Jesus, He won that round of battle. He stood His ground and did not give in to Satan's temptations. He went to Nazareth. He stood in the synagogue. He read the prophecies of the Messiah, and He said, "Today this Scripture is fulfilled in your hearing" (Luke 4:21).

There again, Satan plotted to destroy Jesus. He inspired the hearts of the people to try to kill Jesus. They took hold of Him and forced Him out to the edge of the city of Nazareth, where they planned to throw Him over the side of a cliff. But Jesus disappeared out of their midst.

Later on, when Jesus was out on a little boat on the Sea of Galilee, Satan stirred up a storm and tried to sink the boat. The disciples woke Jesus and cried out, "We're going to perish!" So Jesus stood up and rebuked the wind and the waves—and they obeyed and were still (Luke 8:24).

But Satan wasn't done with Jesus. Next he filled the heart of Judas Iscariot, who knew the Sanhedrin was just looking for a chance to capture Jesus. So Judas came to the high priest and said, "If you'll give me thirty pieces of silver, I'll lead you to Him. I know where He prays." And Judas Iscariot led the high priest's soldiers into the garden of Gethsemane where they arrested Jesus. They took Him back to the house of Caiaphas, condemned Him in a mock trial, and then took Him to Pilate.

Then Satan stirred the hearts of the people with animosity against this Man of love. "Crucify Him! Crucify Him!" they demanded. And their voices prevailed. Pilate turned Jesus over to be crucified.

As Jesus hung dying on the cross, it looked as if the kingdom of darkness had finally triumphed. Darkness covered the land, as if the forces of hell were rejoicing in their great victory.

But early in the morning of the first day of the week, when the women went to the tomb to care for Jesus' body, they found the stone had been rolled away. They searched for Him, but His body was not there—for Jesus had risen from the dead. And in so doing, He had triumphed over Satan, death, and hell. After showing Himself to His disciples, He rose again in triumph to sit at the right hand of the Father until all of His enemies will be made His footstool.

Satan tried to halt God's plan—but Jesus would not let him. Jesus defeated Satan at the cross. Rather than spelling victory for Satan, the cross spelled his defeat through the resurrection of Jesus Christ. And it is by His death on the cross that He redeemed the lost world back to God, and lost men back to God.

However, Satan refused to acknowledge defeat. He continues to ignore his own defeat. Today, as he has done for over two thousand years now, Satan fights to hold on to that which is no longer rightfully his.

You may remember the story of Saul, the first king of Israel in the Old Testament. Saul could have been a great king but he failed to fully obey God's instructions. As a result of his disobedience, Samuel, the prophet of God, came to him and said, "I will not return with you, for you have rejected the word of the LORD, and the LORD has rejected you from being king over Israel ... The LORD has torn the kingdom of Israel from you today, and has given it to a neighbor of yours" (1 Samuel 15:26, 28). Samuel was told to go down to the house of Jesse and anoint one of his sons to be king. He did that, anointing David to be king over Israel.

From that moment on, as far as God was concerned, David was the anointed king. But Saul would not give up the throne. Saul tried hard to hang on to that which was no longer his, even to the point of force.

The same is true of the world. At the cross, Satan was deposed, so the world is no longer rightfully his. But he is stubborn. He will use force if necessary to hang on to that which no longer belongs to him.

Therefore, when we pray over a situation or for a person, we are laying claim to the victory of the cross of Christ. In so doing, we are taking territory back from Satan. And when we come against Satan by way of Christ's victory on the cross, the glorious truth is that *he must yield*. He cannot hold on. He has got to let go. But Satan is relentless. He won't let go easily and he won't yield to anything but prayer.

If we want to tear down Satan's strongholds and pry his fingers off those he has taken captive, we can't go about it haphazardly. We can't toss plastic darts his way and think we are going to send the enemy fleeing.

We need to strategize.

# THE PLAN

## CHAPTER 4

# THE BATTLE PLAN

If we want our prayers to be powerful and effective, if we want our prayers to make a difference in the battle that rages around us, we need to follow a battle plan. We need to employ the following principles:

### MAKE GOD'S WILL THE FOCUS OF YOUR PRAYERS

How do you do this? How do you know how to pray God's will? You discover the will of God through the Word of God. God has declared to you His will, His purpose, and His plan in the pages of the Bible. Give place to the Scriptures in your prayers. As we discussed in chapter 2, all the answers you need for life are found in Scripture. If you make the study of God's Word your habit, you will discover God's will for your life and for any specific problem that arises.

When you pray, freely express your needs, and the needs of those around you to God. Tell Him what you see, what you feel, and what you desire. Then turn to the Word and listen while God speaks to you by His Holy Spirit. He will minister to you and show His will and plan for your life.

## PRAY THROUGH JESUS

After you have listened for awhile by reading His Word, come to Him again with a refocused prayer. "Well, Lord, here it is in Your Word. I can see this is what You desire, so I believe and trust You, in the name of Jesus Christ."

In Genesis 32, when Jacob heard that his brother Esau—who had vowed to kill him—was coming to meet him with four hundred men, Jacob naturally feared for his life. That fear drove him to pray, and as he did so, he reminded God of His promise. He said, "O God of my father Abraham and God of my father Isaac, the LORD who said to me, 'Return to your country and to your family, and I will deal well with you'" (Genesis 32:9). Jacob's prayer was based on that specific promise. He was taking God at His word. But note that Jacob addressed Him as "God of my father Abraham and God of my father Isaac." Jacob approached God on the basis of his ancestors' connection to God.

Today, we have a different, more intimate concept of God. Yes, He is the God of Abraham, Isaac, and Jacob.

But more than that, He is our Father. That is only true because of Jesus Christ. It is true because through His death and resurrection, we have been adopted into God's family. So when we come to God, we can come boldly, with the knowledge that He is our Father. We have that boldness because we know that Jesus Christ is our Intercessor before the Father. Prayer is to be addressed to the Father, in the authority of the name of Jesus.

On our own, we have no right to an audience with God. There is no possible way we could earn such a privilege on our own. That is because we have no part in God's family apart from Jesus Christ. "I am the way, the truth, and the life," He said. "No one comes to the Father except through Me" (John 14:6). And so we need our Intercessor.

Ask the Father for your needs, but ask Him in the name of Jesus Christ. It is only through Christ that you have the right to come, that you have an audience with God, and that you are received. When you knock, use the name of Jesus.

## BE PERSISTENT

Why is persistence necessary in prayer? Some people say that praying for the same need more than once shows a lack of faith on our part. Yet Scripture gives us examples of repeated prayers.

Paul admitted that the thorn in his flesh so disturbed him that, "Concerning this thing I pleaded with the Lord three times that it might depart from me" (2 Corinthians 12:8).

Jesus in the garden of Gethsemane prayed the same prayer three times (Matthew 26:39–44). And He taught persistence in prayer in two parables. In the first one He said that "men always ought to pray and not lose heart" (Luke 18:1). He then illustrated this with the story of a callous judge and a determined widow. The widow visited the judge every day, saying, "Get justice for me from my adversary."

The judge was an unjust man who feared neither God nor man, and yet the woman's persistence wore him down. He eventually wrote out his judgment in her favor. Then Jesus added, "Shall God not avenge His own elect …? I tell you that He will avenge them speedily" (Luke 18:2–8).

People are sometimes troubled with the fact that Jesus used an unjust judge as a comparison with our just God. But the parable actually shows a vast contrast. If an unjust judge could be persuaded to act by the persistence of a woman, how much more will our fair and loving Father bring about a just and speedy judgment for those who call upon Him?

The other parable about persistence in prayer concerns a fellow who heard a knock on his door at midnight. Opening the door, he found that some of his friends had come to spend the night. He wanted to feed them before he bedded them down, so he went to the cupboard to get them some bread—but there wasn't enough. So he went to his neighbor's house, knocked on the door, and said, "Open up and give me some bread! I've got company."

The neighbor replied, "I'm already in bed with my wife and children. Come back tomorrow." But the fellow kept knocking and wouldn't stop until he had what he needed. Because of this man's importunity, the neighbor finally got up and gave him the bread (Luke 11:5–8).

Clearly, the Bible teaches persistence in prayer. Does that mean our prayers persuade God to do things our way? Does God have an arbitrary reluctance to answer us? Do we then make Him give in to our demands by being obnoxiously determined? I hardly think so. I am convinced that prayers do not and cannot change the purposes of God, even if you pray for days, even if you petition with tears. God is far too loving to give in just because you weep and persevere for something He knows would harm or destroy you in the end.

Though prayer doesn't change God's mind or God's purposes, prayer does change something—it changes us. Often as I am praying over a situation, God speaks to me. He sometimes shows me His plan, which is always so much better than what I had in mind. While in prayer, God deals with me and shows me the folly of certain things that I have been insisting upon, and even demanding from Him.

Prayer doesn't change the purpose of God, but prayer can change the *action* of God. Jesus said, "Your Father knows the things you have need of before you ask Him" (Matthew 6:8). Your prayers don't inform God of your situation. He knows all your needs before you ever ask Him. Your prayers open the door so God can do those things He has desired to do, but wouldn't do in violation of your own free will.

How long do you persist in prayer? You pray until you get an answer—either a "yes" or a "no." If the answers to your prayers don't come immediately—don't give up! In the example Paul gave of Epaphras "laboring fervently" in prayer for the Colossians, I think fervently means fervently. I don't believe Epaphras said, "O Lord, bless the church in Colosse. In Jesus' name, amen." Rather, he waited upon God, diligently sought after God for the welfare and the benefit of the church, and *continued* the practice of prayer day after day. As James 5:16 tells us, "The effective, fervent prayer of a righteous man avails much."

One of the mistakes we often make in prayer is thinking too soon that the battle is won. Satan is alarmed, and his grip may have slipped a bit, but he hasn't quite let go. The small inklings of success we see give us the wrong impression. We think we have already won and we can stop fighting. Take, for example, the situation where you are praying for someone who has been making wrong choices, maybe even dangerous choices. The person begins to soften a bit. You hear him say, "Oh, I have been such a fool. I didn't realize the mess I was making of my life. I'm going to change. Things are going to be different from now on." Relieved, you think, "Praise the Lord! That one is finished. Thank God, that person is okay now." And you quit praying—just short of victory.

In his book *How to Win Friends and Influence People*, Dale Carnegie tells of a Mr. Darby, a wealthy insurance broker from the east, who got caught up with gold fever and headed out to Colorado to do some prospecting. As it turned out, he discovered a very rich vein of gold in the Rockies. Returning to the east, he convinced his friends to invest their money in a mining venture. They formed a corporation, bought a great deal of equipment, and mined this very wealthy vein of gold ore in Colorado.

Just about the time the corporation paid off all its debts, the vein of gold ran out. But the investors didn't give up right away. They kept digging until they ran themselves into debt again. Finally one day, a discouraged Mr. Darby ordered an end to the digging. He closed the mine, went into Denver, and sold the mine and equipment to a junk dealer for a few hundred dollars before returning east.

The junk dealer then hired a geologist to study the mine and the area. The geologist came back with this report: "If you'll dig three feet past the point where Mr. Darby quit, you'll find that same vein of gold." Just three feet more! That junk dealer became the wealthiest mine owner in the state of Colorado.

I wonder how many times we, too, stop three feet short of victory. We take those small signs of hope and those initial victories and think the battle is over. But Satan is not finished. He just retreated temporarily, just long enough to devise his counterattack. He is not about to give up that quickly. He will try another strategy to regain that territory from which he has been driven—and he will try it when you are no longer looking because you thought that battle was over.

This is a key principle of our warfare: What we gain through prayer, we must then hold onto through prayer against the power of the enemy. The power of prayer is far greater than Satan's power, but we have got to exercise that weapon if we want to see real and lasting results.

## BE SPECIFIC

Something else you need to realize about our enemy: Satan will only yield specific territory that you have specifically prayed about. There is nothing the enemy loves more than vague, generalized prayers. "Oh God, save the world." That kind of prayer doesn't dent the enemy and it doesn't budge him an inch. But when you bring an individual before the Lord and you begin to pray for that person—praying *specifically* about that person's situation, and laying claim to that person for Jesus Christ—Satan must yield.

"Lord, my friend John is bound by the power of Satan. His life is being ruined and twisted. I come against that work of Satan in the name of Jesus Christ and in the victory of the cross of Jesus Christ. I ask You, Father, to free him from this power of Satan that is gripping him today. Loose him now, that he may know the love of Jesus Christ. Lord, let Your Spirit speak to his heart and bring an end to the work of Satan that is both binding and blinding him."

We must be specific. We have to bring before God life by life, individual by individual, territory by territory—personally, individually, directly, and specifically, to drive the enemy thoroughly and definitively away. When we do that, Satan is defeated. When we bring the power of Jesus' victory on the cross through prayer, Satan has no choice but to yield.

## PRAY WITH ASSURANCE

Prayer is so much more powerful than we realize. Through prayer, we can pull down the very strongholds of the enemy and free our loved ones from Satan's hold. As the Bible tells us, "The weapons of our warfare are not carnal but mighty in God for pulling down strongholds" (2 Corinthians 10:4).

The question arises, "Can I pray with assurance for my unsaved loved ones? After all, we know that God will not save anyone against their will." That is true. God will not save you against your will. If you do not want to be saved, don't worry. God is not going to save you. He has given you free will and He will never save you against your will.

Jesus said, "Behold, I stand at the door and knock" (Revelation 3:20). Jesus stands at the door and He knocks. Note that He is not pounding to get in. You don't have to worry about Him busting the door down if you don't answer. He said, "If anyone hears My voice and opens the door.... " That is what's needed. God will not force entry into your life. You've got to open the door.

So, if God won't force a person against their will, how then can I pray with assurance that God will save them?

You have to remember the truth of an unbeliever's condition, and you must understand the nature of the battle. You see, your unsaved loved one is not really free to make a choice about his or her salvation, because Satan is holding them in his grip.

Regarding those who are unsaved—those who are in opposition to God—Paul encouraged Timothy to correct them in humility, "if God perhaps will grant them repentance, so that they may know the truth, and that they may come to their senses and escape the snare of the devil, having been taken captive by him to do his will" (2 Timothy 2:25-26). Those under Satan's control have no choice but to do his bidding, and they have no hope of escape without intervention by God.

Those Satan ensnares, he also blinds. Paul described those who are perishing as those "whose minds the god of this age has blinded, who do not believe, lest the light of the gospel of the glory of Christ, who is the image of

God, should shine on them" (2 Corinthians 4:4). That unbelieving loved one of yours can't receive, because they can't see the truth. Satan has blinded their eyes and is holding them in his power. Therefore, your prayers must be directed against Satan's power.

When you bring a person before the Lord and in the victory of Jesus Christ upon the cross, you are commanding that Satan release the hold he has upon their life. Jesus died to redeem us. Jesus won the victory. He has already purchased our salvation, so Satan's power is an usurped power over the lives of the unsaved. He has no real right to them. When we understand that, we can demand that he release them from the hold he has over them. And the beautiful thing is that Satan must let go. He can't hold on any longer.

Through Christ, we can demand that Satan free our loved ones from the blindness that has so perverted their thinking towards the gospel and given them such a jaundiced view of Jesus Christ. We can demand that they be set free from what has blinded them to the truth and to the reality of their own need.

I remember a man once telling me, "You know, it is amazing. When I was an alcoholic and a drug addict, I didn't realize what a mess I had made of my life. I thought I was cool. I thought I was really living. I thought things were going great." He said, "I was completely blind to the fact that I was destroying my marriage and everything else in my life. I just didn't see it."

It could be that you know others like this man who are totally blind to their reality today. The god of this world has blinded their eyes so that they cannot see the truth.

By prayer you can come against that blinding work of Satan that has kept them from seeing the truth. By prayer you can open their eyes and their hearts that they might realize the mess their life is in and that they might see the need they have for God, even though they may not even believe in God. Why don't they believe? It is because Satan has blinded their eyes to truth.

Once a person has been truly freed from Satan's grip and can finally see the truth, the rational, reasonable, logical response is to then receive Jesus as their Lord. At that point, only a fool would reject Him. So if your loved ones aren't fools, you can have great hope. You can pray for them with assurance. I have seen it happen time and time again. The Lord said, "Come now, and let us reason together" (Isaiah 1:18). It is reasonable to accept the cleansing God offers. But when their minds are clogged by Satan's work and power, they can't reason.

So we've got to pray for those living in darkness around us. When we see a glimmer of hope, we've got to keep on praying. The battle is not yet won. It is won only when Satan finally yields back that territory he has been holding on to—that territory he no longer has a right to hold. But he will yield it only when we demand, through prayer, that he do so.

From time to time, people ask me, "Is it right to pray more than once for the same thing? If I have enough faith, can I just pray once and that's enough?"

We have already discussed persistence as it relates to God. But when we realize the effect continued prayer has on Satan, we realize anew the need for persistence. Prayer is an assault against the strongholds of the enemy, and every prayer becomes a fresh blow against his grip. Every prayer breaks down the resistance he has created. So, repeated prayers are necessary as we storm the fortresses of darkness, and as we deliver people from the kingdom of darkness that they might come into the glorious light of the love of God in Christ Jesus.

By now you should be seeing that you have the power to set your friends and loved ones free from the work of Satan that has bound them and blinded them. You have the power to free them in order that they might make a free choice and find the glorious light of the gospel and the love of Christ. The reason why they are going on in darkness is that no one has taken the time or the effort to get into the battle and fight for them. We must recognize that we come from a position of strength, power, and victory, because that battle has already been fought and won. All we have to do is lay claim to that victory—life after life, situation after situation.

It is time we begin to set the world free around us. Satan's had his day much too long. It is time that the church quit singing, "Hold the fort," and start singing, "Storm the fort, for God is with us!" We need to get out in the trenches and begin to slug it out. It is time for us to take away the territory Satan is trying to hold and to set at liberty those being held captive—for God's sake, for their sake, and for the world's sake.

I would like to pray for that right now.

> *Father, we come to You in Jesus' name, in the authority and the power that has been given to us. Lord, we bring before You those areas of our own lives where Satan has defeated us, especially this area of prayer where he has kept us from exercising the power and the authority that is ours. We have given up too soon, Lord. We have let ourselves be talked out of continued prayer. "It's too much," we say, or "That person will never change." But we see now, Lord, that when we do that we have just granted Satan territory that doesn't belong to him and we have allowed him to rule. Oh God, spur us to pray. Ignite in us a passion to pray for the lost. In Jesus' name, may we begin to set at liberty those who are bound and blinded—to Your glory. Amen.*

James cautioned us to "Be doers of the word, and not hearers only" (James 1:22). I don't want you to go away saying, "Isn't this power we have marvelous? How good of Jesus to have won the victory for us! It is so glorious and exciting. I'm truly stirred." Saying it is not enough. No, I want you to *do* something.

Pray. Set your friends free. Watch God work. Come against the enemy and demand that he back off. He has to. He cannot hold on when you come against him in the victory of the cross of Christ. He has to let go. Begin to force him off of that territory. Begin to lay claim to your loved ones for God. Set them free. Ask God to open their eyes that they might find the glorious light of the gospel in the face of Jesus Christ.

Yes, we are in a war—but the good news is our Savior has won it already. For now, we must fight the battles on behalf of our friends and loved ones by reclaiming the territory Satan has taken. And we do that through the amazing power of prayer. Let us take up our weapons daily on their behalf.

## Carnal Means versus Spiritual Means

Though we can't see the spirit world, we can definitely feel the effects of the battle raging there. We might feel disturbed, despondent, depressed, or even oppressed. But sometimes that is all we say—"I feel upset," or "I feel irritable." We don't recognize that there may be spiritual forces behind the conflict we are feeling, and so we don't engage in spiritual battle.

Many years ago, on a Saturday morning, I discovered something very interesting. When all our children were younger and still living in our home, some mornings were difficult. There just seemed to be a spirit of irritability or agitation that would cause the children to grate on each other. They would call each other names and bicker back and forth, until finally I would jump in and begin directing each one. "All right, you go to your room," to one and, "You empty the trash," to another, and to the third, "You go do the dishes." One by one, they would go off to their various tasks mumbling under their breath, but clearly still carrying with them this spirit of agitation. As they would go, they would cast their last little barb at the other one. It truly upset the home—and of course, it usually happened when I was trying to do my study and get my Sunday morning message ready.

Then one particular Saturday morning, something different happened. I remember it well, because it brought a real change into my own life. As I was reading the Word and waiting upon the Lord, I heard the kids going at it with each other. The same irritation began to rise within me as the names they called each other became more pointed. The agitation began to swell and before I knew it, I was upset. Like always, I started to put down my Bible and go jump in the middle of the fray.

But just then the Lord spoke to my heart. He said, "This is a spiritual battle. It is spiritual warfare. Now, take dominion over it in the realm of the Spirit. Just sit here and take dominion over this in the name of Jesus and watch Me work."

So I said, "Father, I come against this spirit of agitation in the heart of the kids this morning. I stand against it in the name of Jesus. Father, I pray that You'll bring a love into their hearts and a peace into the house, and that You'll bind this work of the enemy that is trying to disrupt our home."

Before I had even finished my prayer, one of the kids made a joke and they all started laughing together. Within seconds, the whole tenor, the whole mood, the whole atmosphere had changed in our house. Instead of the usual contention, the attitude in the home had mellowed out.

The Lord taught me an extremely important lesson that morning. He reminded me that the battle is spiritual, so we have to employ spiritual weapons. Carnal weapons simply do not work in such a battle. But we frequently try to use physical means to deal with those spiritual issues.

Unfortunately, the church has frequently led the way in this wrong thinking—in trying to accomplish spiritual ends with carnal means. The old adage, "The end justifies the means," isn't scriptural, and it isn't right. But how many churches have bought into that philosophy? It is carnal for a church to adopt Madison Avenue techniques in order to meet its budget. Yet so many churches have been caught in that trap. They establish their church budget, figuring what they will need to get through the year, and then form a committee. Then this committee goes out in groups of two or three—just to make sure they have a psychological edge—and has a home visit with every member of the church. They ask each to make a faith pledge to the church for the coming year, encouraging them, "This year, do a little more." Once a faith pledge has been solicited, the member's name and pledge amount is put in the computer for tracking. If a member falls behind, a letter is automatically sent out. "You are behind in your faith pledge. We established our budget trusting that you would be making your payments. And now unless you come through and rescue the church, we are going to have to cut back on some of our events."

I say this with absolute certainty: God never intended the church to accomplish spiritual ends through carnal means.

My break with the denomination I was serving years ago came over this very issue. While in a conference in Phoenix, Arizona, the bishop stood up and said, "Now, I know that to motivate people through competition is using carnal motivation. But we must face the fact that the majority of the people we minister to are carnal—so it is necessary to use carnal motivation." When I heard this, I said in my heart, "I can't. I won't. It's not right. If the majority of the people are carnal, then it is our duty as pastors to lead them into a spiritual relationship with God, rather than to pander to their carnality." From that moment on, I knew I could not serve God within that denomination.

It seems so obviously wrong when it is spelled out that way, so blatant. Yet many churches continue to make this tragic mistake—using carnal methods to promote the program of God. The problem is, once you start using these carnal means, you've got to continue using them. If you develop a crowd through promotion and sensationalism, you can't ever stop. You have to keep it up in order to keep the crowd. If you strive to gain, then you have to strive to maintain.

That is why so many churches are in trouble. They have tried every gimmick in the world. They have developed their program through this big push, this big drive, this big event, this big striving—and now they've got to keep the momentum going or the whole thing will die.

The beautiful thing about watching God work and letting the Spirit do what He wants in your church is that when you don't strive to gain, you don't have to strive to maintain. It is God's work from start to finish. He began it and He will keep it going.

What is true of the church is true of you. No matter what task lies before you, no matter what mountain looms ahead, you have two choices: you can try to accomplish it through carnal means, or through spiritual. You can use physical weapons—weapons wielded in the flesh and limited by the flesh—or you can use the weapons of warfare Paul referred to in 2 Corinthians 10:4—weapons powerful enough to pull down strongholds—and send Satan and his demons fleeing.

The choice seems clear to me.

## THE SPIRIT NATURE OF PRAYER

It is difficult to fight a spiritual battle when we are trapped in physical bodies. These tents of flesh are a great encumbrance in battle. But something amazing happens when we pray—our prayers take on the nature of a spirit.

Let me give you an example. Not long ago on a Sunday morning, my body was in Jerusalem, but my mind was set on my church in Costa Mesa. You see, Sunday night in Israel is Sunday morning back home. I still had my watch set to California time, so I was aware of what was happening at the church. I was thoroughly enjoying my visit in Israel, but I must confess that I was missing home and wishing I could be with everyone at church. So I kept checking the time and waiting for each service to start, and as each did, I would pray that God's blessings would be upon those who were ministering His Word in my absence. I prayed also that the hearts of the people would be open to receive God's truth, and that God would do a mighty work in the fellowship that morning.

It took many long hours on a rough, uncomfortable plane ride to get my body back to Costa Mesa after that trip. But my spirit? That is another story. The body may be limited by time, space, and material objects, but through prayer, our spirits can instantly be anywhere in the world joining with God in His work.

Think about the spirits we know as angels. Did you know that when you gather with your church on Sunday mornings, it is more than likely that angels join you? It's true. The Bible tells us in 1 Peter 1:12 that angels long to look into the mysteries of the gospel. They are curious about the redeemed and about the things God has proposed for His people.

God has work for His angels all over the world, so they don't stay in one place indefinitely. It is possible that an angel visiting your church was across the country—or even across the world—just minutes before. They are not constrained by time the way we are. And though we have to walk through the doors of the church to get inside, angels can get in through the floor, the ceiling, or the walls. Nothing hinders angels. They are not constrained by material objects.

And neither are our prayers. Just like spirit beings, our prayers are completely unhindered. Through prayer, you can be on one side of the world and spiritually join with someone on the other side of the world. You can pray blessings on them; you can pray for their protection, you can pray that God strengthens them for the spiritual battle they are facing. It is marvelous. Prayer is a tremendous tool, a mighty weapon.

## THE BATTLEGROUND

Prayer is a spiritual activity that utilizes both our spirit and our mind. As Paul said in 1 Corinthians 14:15, "I will pray with the spirit, and I will also pray with the understanding." Other versions say, "... and I will also pray with my mind." Herein lies a concern. In his second letter to the Corinthians, Paul highlighted a problem with the mind: "Casting down arguments and every high thing that exalts itself against the knowledge of God, bringing every thought into captivity to the obedience of Christ" (2 Corinthians 10:5).

The battleground—the place where Satan wages his war against God—is your mind. Satan attacks us through our thoughts and our imagination. He wants nothing more than to bring you into spiritual bondage and defeat, and your mind is a convenient and efficient tool he uses to achieve that goal.

There is a law of metaphysics known as visualization. The belief behind visualization is that if you want something, you just need to visualize yourself as already having it. Maybe you want a million dollars. Proponents of visualization would tell you to imagine that you already have that million dollars. Visualize all the things you would own if you had that money—the kind of car you would drive, the house you would live in, and the clothes you would wear. According to the law of metaphysics, by visualizing yourself in the situations you desire, you are actually planting the desire into your subconscious mind. Once those goals are planted, your subconscious mind works away twenty-four hours a day, devising schemes and methods whereby your visualization may become actualization in your life.

You may have heard of books like *Think and Grow Rich* by Napoleon Hill, or *The Richest Man in Babylon* by George Clason. All these books and philosophies espouse the same metaphysical principles of visualization. Set the goal in your mind and allow your subconscious to work on it until it becomes an actuality.

Satan loves to use tactics like visualization because when we employ that principle, we partner ourselves with him in his scheme to bring us down. Think of how many marriages have been destroyed because one person began fantasizing about someone who was not their spouse. It always begins with visualization—wondering, dreaming, and imagining what it would be like to be in that other relationship. That visualization plants the goal in your subconscious, which works on it until it becomes actuality. What seems like harmless fantasy will lead you straight into bondage. Don't let Satan lure you this way. It is so critical that we learn to cast down these imaginations, and every high thing that would exalt itself against God, against the Word of God, and against the path of God. Do not allow yourself to be carried away in fantasizing or visualizing things God never meant for you to have.

"Bringing every thought into captivity to the obedience of Christ," Paul wrote. When Satan whispers, "Did God really say that? Are you sure He really cares for you? Would it really harm you to enjoy yourself in this way?" we have to take those thoughts captive and hand them over to Jesus Christ. Satan will try his hardest to plant destructive thoughts in your mind. But God, who is greater, has given us the power by His Spirit, the power of the Word, and the power of prayer that we might stand against the wiles of our enemy and fight him in the battle-ground of the mind.

## THE VICTORY

In all this talk of battles and armor and weaponry, it is good to be reminded once again that there is no question about the outcome of this war. It has already been won. Colossians 2:15 says this about Christ's victory on the cross: "Having disarmed principalities and powers, He made a public spectacle of them, triumphing over them in it." Jesus wrought a complete and total victory on the cross. He has routed the enemy—once and for all.

The problem is that Satan is the master of *chutzpah*. He enters in where he doesn't have any right or authority to do so. He establishes strongholds where he has no right being, and he will remain in those strongholds until he is forced out. But we can, through the authority of the name of Jesus and through the victory of the cross of Christ, come against every stronghold that Satan establishes and we can demand that he leave. And when we do—he must vacate the premises. He must. No questions. He must because he has no recourse but to yield to that complete victory wrought for us by Jesus upon the cross.

Jesus is the rightful King over this world. The word *Messiah* means "the anointed One." God has anointed Jesus the King. But Satan is still sitting on the throne and doing his best by force to hold on to that which is no longer his. Because of what Jesus did for us on the cross, through prayer we can lay claim to the territory Satan is trying to grab. We can come against that power of the enemy, whether it be in the lives of our family, our children, a husband, or other loved ones or friends. Through Christ's power, we can stand against the enemy and put an end to his blinding work. We can put an end to the hold he has on those we love.

We have been given the weapons we need to free those who are in bondage. It is our privilege and our right to stand in the gap for those who are lost, to lift them up in prayer, and to demand back the territory Satan has stolen inch by inch. Through the power God has given us, we can and should use prayer to set our loved ones free.

And God help us if we don't.

CHAPTER 5

# EXAMPLES OF PRAYER

We have seen that the purpose of prayer is to worship, to petition, to intercede, and to do battle. We have looked at the nature of the war and specific strategies for effective praying, and the importance of taking our thoughts captive. The question then becomes, "How—on a practical level—do we go about praying?"

God has given us many examples in Scripture of prayers and the people who prayed them. Of those many examples, in this chapter we will focus on three: Jesus, the disciples (in Acts 4), and Jabez. We will begin with Jesus and the model prayer He left us in Matthew chapter 6—the prayer we refer to today as "The Lord's Prayer."

## THE LORD'S PRAYER

In Luke chapter 11, we find Jesus praying, as He so often did. Apparently His disciples were nearby, watching. Verse 1 tells us that one of them approached Him with a request, "Lord, teach us to pray." And He did. Both Luke chapter 11 and Matthew chapter 6 give us an account of the prayer that followed.

### Our Father

> "*In* this manner, therefore, pray: Our Father in heaven, hallowed be Your name " (Matthew 6:9).

From the first line of that prayer, we find one vital element for effective prayer: a close personal relationship between the petitioner and God.

Your relationship to God is often manifested in the way you address Him. Some people begin their prayers with "Almighty God," or "Eternal God." Often people who do not yet know Him as their Father address Him in this more formal way. That title often changes from "Almighty God" to "Heavenly Father" when the truth of 1 John 3:1 sinks in: "Behold what manner of love the Father has bestowed on us, that we should be called children of God!"

Think of it! We have been called children of God. I can now come to Him and say, "Father!"

Only through Jesus Christ can we be sons and daughters. Those outside of Jesus Christ have a distant relationship to the almighty, eternal God. But you, through Jesus Christ, can come into an intimate relationship. John said, "As many as received Him, to them He gave the right to become children of God, to those who believe in His name" (John 1:12). And Paul agreed, writing that God has given each of us "the Spirit of adoption by whom we cry out, 'Abba, Father.' The Spirit Himself bears witness with our spirit that we are children of God" (Romans 8:15-16). Because I am His child, I naturally call Him "Father." Relationship is of vital importance in prayer.

"Our Father in heaven" tells us that, first of all, prayer is for the children. It is the privilege of the children to come to the Father. And it is the recognition of the fact that He is a caring, loving Father in heaven.

*Hallowed be Your name.*

Jesus continues His model prayer with praise and worship: "Hallowed be Your name" (Matthew 6:9).

Worship is an important part of prayer. The psalmist told us we are to, "Enter into His gates with thanksgiving, and into His courts with praise" (Psalm 100:4).

Too often we just rush right in and blurt out our requests. To enrich your prayer life, spend some time praising God first.

*Your kingdom come. Your will be done ...*

The first two petitions in Jesus' model prayer are in the

form of intercession: "Your kingdom come. Your will be done ... " (Matthew 6:10).

Later, in the Sermon on the Mount, Jesus said, "But seek first the kingdom of God and His righteousness, and all these things [that you are so often praying about] shall be added to you" (Matthew 6:33).

You know, we fret and worry about so many unnecessary things. The things themselves might be necessary, but the worry is not. That is because God is aware of our needs long before we are, and He is capable of taking care of those needs for us.

Just a few verses earlier, Jesus made a point of this. "Why do you worry about clothing? Consider the lilies of the field, how they grow: they neither toil nor spin; and yet I say to you that even Solomon in all his glory was not arrayed like one of these" (Matthew 6:28-29).

The flowers of the field don't spin wool or cotton into threads to make their coverings. Yet, think of their beauty! Jesus said that even Solomon, who had great wealth and the finest clothing, could not compare to the beauty of the flowers God dressed and placed in the fields.

I wonder if Jesus gestured toward the fields when He said this. There in Israel, the spring wild flowers are just absolutely breathtaking. The hillsides are completely carpeted in beautiful colors. But their beauty doesn't last forever. The season for wild flowers is usually just a month or so. Then, as spring turns into summer, they die quickly and the hills turn brown. Yet God, knowing how brief their appearance will be, still clothes them beautifully.

Jesus uses that fact to make a point. "Now if God so clothes the grass of the field, which today is, and tomorrow is thrown into the oven, will He not much more clothe you, O you of little faith? Therefore do not worry, saying, 'What shall we eat?' or 'What shall we drink?' or 'What shall we wear?' For after all these things the Gentiles [or the heathen] seek. For your heavenly Father knows that you need all these things" (Matthew 6:30-32).

You don't have to worry about these things. And you don't have to worry about those other things that consume your thoughts; things like, "Will I ever get married?" and "Who does God have for me to spend my future with?" Some of you worry greatly about that. But if God is aware of all your needs, don't you think He is aware of that need as well? Trust God. He will take care of you. As David said, "I have been young, and now am old; yet I have not seen the righteous forsaken, nor his descendants begging bread" (Psalm 37:25).

Jesus said, "But seek first the kingdom of God and His righteousness, and all these things shall be added to you. Therefore do not worry about tomorrow, for tomorrow will worry about its own things. Sufficient for the day is its own trouble" (Matthew 6:33-34).

Usually, our worry is concerned with what lies ahead. We worry about tomorrow, or next week, or next month. We don't worry too much about today because today is usually covered. What we need to realize is that God is already there. He has already gone ahead of us and taken care of whatever we are going to encounter.

I can't help but think of the women on the way to the tomb that long-ago Sunday morning. Their plan was to anoint the body of Jesus, but they didn't realize that God had already gone before them and performed a miracle. As they walked, they began to worry. "Who is going to roll away the stone?" The stone that blocked Jesus' tomb was too heavy for them to move it. They probably fretted about that all the way there, not realizing that God had already gone ahead of them. Sure enough, when they reached the tomb, the stone was already rolled away—and Jesus was risen.

So often that is true of our own worries. By the time we get there, it's gone. All that fretting proved to be futile. So Jesus says, "Don't worry about tomorrow." Take care of whatever is before you today. And the Lord, who saw you through today, will see you through tomorrow. Because He is faithful, He will see you through next week, and next month, and next year.

So if we don't need to worry about what we eat, or what we drink, or what we wear, or who we are going to marry, or what is going to happen tomorrow or next week or a year from now; then what should we be concerned about? God's kingdom. "Seek first the kingdom of God and His righteousness, and all these things shall be added to you."

When we pray, our first desire and primary interest should be, "Lord, let Your kingdom come. Let Your will be done … "

*Here on this earth, even as it is in heaven.*

Let us pray, "Lord, bring an end to the ungodly reign of Satan over the earth. Establish Your kingdom, Lord, in my heart and on this earth."

*Give us this day our daily bread.*

After praising God and lifting up His interests, we can then move on to our own needs. Does that contradict our discussion about food, and drink, and clothing? Not at all. There is a difference between bringing your needs to God and laying them at His feet, and simply fretting and stewing over them.

Jesus tells us to pray, "Give us this day our daily bread" (Matthew 6:11). There's nothing wrong with personal petition. "The hardworking farmer must be first to partake of the crops" (2 Timothy 2:6). The fact is, you can't give to others what you have not first received. I cannot impart to others what I do not have myself. Therefore, I must first be a partaker of God's grace, love, strength, and power. Then, as I partake, I have something to share with others.

*And forgive us our debts, as we forgive our debtors.*

In verse 12, Jesus told us to pray, "Forgive us our debts, as we forgive our debtors." Then two verses later, after He concluded His model prayer, Jesus touched on the theme of forgiveness again, emphasizing its importance: "For if you forgive men their trespasses, your heavenly Father will also forgive you. But if you do not forgive men their trespasses, neither will your Father forgive your trespasses" (Matthew 6:14-15).

This means exactly what it says—that if you forgive men their trespasses, your heavenly Father will forgive you. But if you do not forgive men their trespasses, neither will your Father forgive your trespasses.

It is just that simple. Forgiveness is so important to Jesus that it was a common theme in His teaching and ministry. It matters to Him that we understand this vital message: God has forgiven us so much—surely we do not have the right to hold little grievances against our brothers.

Remember the story in Matthew 18 about the servant who owed his master ten thousand talents? In today's terms, that is some ten million dollars—basically, an impossible amount of money. When the master sent for him, the servant said, "Oh, I can't pay you now, but give me a little time and I'll see what I can do."

So the master said, "Oh, let's forget it. I'll write off the debt." And he forgave him the debt that he owed.

So then the servant went out and got hold of a fellow servant who owed him a small debt, maybe sixteen bucks. He said to him, "You have owed me for a long time. I want payment now."

The other servant said, "Oh, I can't pay you now. Give me a week."

But the servant whose huge debt had been forgiven said, "Throw him into prison!" And he had the man jailed for the sixteen-dollar debt.

When the master who had forgiven his servant the huge debt heard of how he had been so hard on his fellow servant, he called the man in and said, "How much did you owe me?"

"Ten million dollars."

"I forgave you the debt, didn't I?"

"Yes."

"How is it that I hear you had a fellow servant thrown into debtors' prison for a sixteen-dollar debt?"

Then the master said, "Throw him into the prison until he has paid the last penny."

Jesus makes the illustration almost ludicrous in order to clarify an important point. He wants us to see that compared to how much we have been forgiven—which would be an impossible debt for us to ever repay—it makes no sense for us to hold such small things against our brothers.

*And do not lead us into temptation, but deliver us from the evil one. For Yours is the kingdom and the power and the glory forever. Amen.*

Jesus starts His prayer with God, and He ends it by bringing it full circle. After asking for protection from temptation, He concludes by praying, "For Yours is the kingdom and the power and the glory forever" (Matthew 6:13).

It all belongs to God. The world is His, the power is His, and every bit of honor and glory is His. As we pray, we are not reminding God of this fact—we are reminding ourselves. All that we have comes from Him and all that we do is for His glory alone.

In prayer, you can come to God and present your requests to Him. You can open your heart to Him and lay bare the innermost secrets of your soul. You can talk with your Father and find the strength and guidance you need.

What a blessing prayer is! May God help you to discover the full, amazing experience of prayer—not as a work, not as a task, not as a duty, not as a burden, not as an obligation—but as the most joyous privilege in the world!

## THE DISCIPLES' PRAYER

In the third chapter of Acts, Peter and John healed a lame man at the gate of the temple called "Beautiful." As the healed man began leaping and praising God, he attracted the attention of a crowd—some five thousand people.

Noting their amazement, Peter took the opportunity to share the gospel with them. This upset the rulers—the priests, the elders, and the scribes. They didn't like that the man was healed, and they didn't like that Peter had lifted up the name of Jesus.

So the magistrates called the disciples in for questioning and asked, "By what power or by what name have you done this?" (Acts 4:7).

Then Peter, filled with the Holy Spirit, answered with this powerful speech: "Rulers of the people and elders of Israel: If we this day are judged for a good deed done to a helpless man, by what means he has been made well, let it be known to you all, and to all the people of Israel, that by the name of Jesus Christ of Nazareth, whom you crucified, whom God raised from the dead, by Him this man stands here before you whole. This is the 'stone which was rejected by you builders, which has become the chief cornerstone.' Nor is there salvation in any other, for there is no other name under heaven given among men by which we must be saved" (Acts 4:8-12).

Beautiful. But the rulers of Israel didn't see it that way. Afraid that Peter's boldness and his message might spread to the people, they threatened the disciples with dire consequences if they continued preaching about Jesus; and, in fact, commanded the disciples to stop speaking the name of Jesus altogether.

But Peter and John made their intentions clear. "Whether it is right in the sight of God to listen to you more than to God, you judge. For we cannot but speak the things which we have seen and heard" (Acts 4:19-20).

The magistrates threatened them further, and then let them go. Peter and John immediately went back to the church and they shared with those in the church of the threats that they had received from the earthly magistrates. And so the church got together and prayed: "Lord, You are God, who made heaven and earth and the sea, and all that is in them ... " (Acts 4:24).

The disciples had just had this harrowing experience, but you will note that they didn't begin their prayer with a request for strength—they began their prayer with a recognition of the greatness of God. That is just what we observed about the Lord's Prayer—Jesus, too, began His prayer by proclaiming God's greatness.

They then acknowledged their trial did not take God by surprise. God already knew about the situation—in fact, He knew about it a thousand years earlier and had inspired David to write about it. "... who by the mouth of Your servant David have said: 'Why did the nations rage, and the people plot vain things? The kings of the earth took their stand, and the rulers were gathered together against the LORD and against His Christ.' For truly against Your holy Servant Jesus, whom You anointed, both Herod and Pontius Pilate, with the Gentiles and the people of Israel, were gathered together to do whatever Your hand and Your purpose determined before to be done" (Acts 4:25-28).

When you have acknowledged God's greatness and His omniscience, you are finally in the right place. You've got the right perspective to make your request. "Now, Lord, look on their threats, and grant to Your servants that with all boldness they may speak Your word, by stretching out Your hand to heal, and that signs and wonders may be done through the name of Your holy Servant Jesus" (Acts 4:29-30).

"They are trying to silence us, Lord. They want to stop us from using Your name. But we ask for boldness. Don't let them stop Your work." I find this beautiful. They are asking God for the boldness to keep on doing the very thing that got them into trouble in the first place.

As a response to this prayer, three things happened. First, we read in Acts 4:31, "And when they had prayed, the place where they were assembled together was shaken...."

That is a powerful prayer. It reminds me of years ago when I was in Bible college and had been elected as the student body president. One of my functions was to lead the student prayer meeting every morning before school. Then, after various students had prayed, I would close in prayer and dismiss them to their classes.

This one particular evening, while studying this particular fourth chapter of Acts, I was impressed by the fact that after they prayed, "the place was shaken." I thought,

"Wow, that is real power in prayer." Think of praying and then having the place shake on you!

The next morning at our student prayer meeting, I was leading the closing prayer and getting ready to dismiss the students to class, when I began feeling the pulpit shaking back and forth. For a split second, I thought, "Amazing! I just read this last night." But then pretty quickly I realized it was just one of those California earthquakes.

The second thing that God did in response to their prayer was, "they were all filled with the Holy Spirit." And thirdly, "they spoke the word of God with boldness" (Acts 4:31).

They meditated on God's greatness. They acknowledged that God knew all their troubles before any came to be. They asked to be part of His work. And the Lord answered their prayer.

## THE PRAYER OF JABEZ

I am always interested in the prayers we find in the Bible. And I am especially interested in those prayers that produced results. The prayer of Jabez in the Old Testament is one such example. In studying his words, we can learn some valuable insights into prayer. For example, Jabez calls us to answer the question, "Which god do you serve?"

The Bible declares that when Jabez prayed, he "called on the God of Israel" (1 Chronicles 4:10). What god do you call upon when you pray?

Over the years, I have met people whose lives appear to be careless, reckless, and sinful. When we start talking and they realize that I am a minister, they usually say something like, "I know I'm not living the way I should, but I pray every single night. I never go to sleep without first saying my prayers."

That always makes me wonder. When these people pray, "Now I lay me down to sleep, I pray Thee, Lord ... " to whom are they addressing their rote prayer? Who is the true lord of their lives?

"Lord" is not so much a name as it is a title. People serve many different gods, many different lords. Who is the lord of your life? It is important to know the one you are addressing in your prayers. Jesus said that "not all who say, 'Lord, Lord,' are going to enter the kingdom of heaven" (Matthew 7:21).

Israel couldn't seem to make up their mind whom they wanted to serve. They had gone after numerous other gods—*Baal, Molech, Ashtoreth*, to name a few. Finally, God told Jeremiah that He would no longer hear the children of Israel when they called on Him. He told Jeremiah to tell the people that they weren't to call on Him when calamity came, but should "go and cry out to the gods to whom they offer incense" (Jeremiah 11:12). Let them call on the gods they had been serving.

It is a tragic day when God finally says, "I have had it! You have worshiped and served everything but Me. The only time I hear from you is when you are in trouble. So the next time you find yourself in trouble, try calling on the gods you prefer to serve."

Not many people serve gods with names like *Baal, Molech, Ashtoreth,* or *Mammon* these days. Instead, they worship gods with sophisticated names—names like "intellect" or "pleasure" or "power" or "money." They may not realize they have chosen a god for themselves, but that is precisely what they have done. Whatever your supreme passion is, that is your god.

For example, some people refuse to accept the notion of a supreme being because they can't understand it with their intellect. They will only accept those things they can understand with their minds. To them, knowledge is the goal. To know, to understand, is the highest achievement. Thus, their god is intellect.

Some spend their whole lives pursuing love, romance, and passion. They think love is the ultimate aim of life. Sometimes they even identify themselves this way—"I'm a lover!" If you asked them, "Who is your god?" It is unlikely they would answer, "I serve *Venus,* the goddess of love." But that is exactly who they serve. And when trouble comes and they feel a need to cry out to God, they may as well cry out, "Oh, *Venus*! Save me!" Because that is the god they serve.

Others serve pleasure. They live and work the entire week long with one thought on their minds: the weekend.

"Friday night we'll take the camper, the three-wheeler, and the boat, and we'll head up to the river. What a weekend we'll have!" All week long they are preparing and tinkering and readying themselves for their god: pleasure. But if you asked them the name of their god, they wouldn't ever think to say, "*Molech*. I serve the god of pleasure." Yet in reality, that ancient god is the one they have chosen for themselves.

And then let us not forget those who love money—and all the power and possessions money can buy. These people scheme constantly to find ways to get more money so they can acquire more possessions. Their minds are always analyzing how to cut this, increase that, invest here or there. They take second jobs. They read about money, think about money, dream about money. Guess who their god is—money. In ancient terms, that god is *Mammon*. When these people finally face something they can't buy off, something they are helpless to tackle by themselves, they cry out, "Oh God, help me!" But their god *Mammon* can't hear.

Don't ever forget that the prospect of your prayers being answered is totally dependent upon the one whom you petition. You might come to me and say, "Chuck, I need one hundred thousand dollars. I am desperate. If I don't get one hundred thousand dollars, I don't know what I am going to do!"

You could plead with me for a week, two weeks, or two years—but you don't have a chance of getting that from me. I just don't have it. You are petitioning someone who has no power or capacity to answer.

The prophets of *Baal* cried out to him all morning to send fire to their altar, and they never received an answer. That is because *Baal* is an impotent god. He had no capacity to answer. And neither does the god of intellect, the god of love, the god of pleasure, or the god of money.

In the hour of real need, these gods can produce nothing. But when I cry out to *Jehovah*, the God of Israel, I know that He is able to do far more abundantly than all I could ask or think. There is no end to God's power. When I cry out to Him, He is able to meet all my needs. "One hundred thousand dollars?" He asks. "Is that all?"

How empty life is when you serve an impersonal, impotent god. I have stood beside many such people in their time of need. When their child is lying on a hospital bed and the doctor walks out of the operating room shaking his head, they look at me as if to say, "Do something, preacher!" Their god is silent when they need him most.

But when you worship *Jehovah*, He is there at your call. He is able to help in your hour of need.


PETITIONS OF JABEZ

Jabez knew whom he served. When he cried out, "Oh God!" he wasn't just throwing a title at the sky. Jabez was calling upon the God of Israel, saying, "Oh, that You would bless me indeed" (1 Chronicles 4:10). Jabez wasn't ashamed to say, "Bless me." I am not ashamed to ask God to bless me, either. I want every blessing that God has for me. If I am to be a blessing to others, I must first receive the blessings of God.

Now notice the blessings that Jabez requested in this simple little prayer, found in 1 Chronicles 4:10.

His second request was, "Enlarge my territory." Though the Jews had entered the Promised Land, much of the land was still in the hands of the enemy. God had promised them the entire land, but they had not yet obtained the full promise of God. Thus Jabez prayed, "Lord, enlarge my territory," or actually, "Help me to possess all that You have given me."

I pray this in my own life. "Lord," I pray, "help me to possess all that You have given and promised to me."

God has given us rich and precious promises. In Christ Jesus, we live in the heavenlies. Through Him, we can live in a glorious spiritual atmosphere. But instead we choose to drag along on the bottom of the pile, groveling in the dirt. You may enjoy it down here, but I enjoy it up there. Thus I pray, "Lord, bless me and help me to possess all that You have given to me. I thank You for what You have already done for me, Lord, but You have promised so much more...."

After all, why should you close the door on what God wants to do for you? Some people say, "I really don't feel

I need the gifts of the Spirit." Personally, I need everything that God has to give me. Not only do I *need* everything that God has offered to give me, I *desire* everything that He has to give.

When I come to God, I don't close any doors. I say, "Lord, here I am. Do things Your way. Don't let me put any restrictions in Your path. Enlarge my coast, and allow me to possess all that You have promised." Whenever I try to dictate to God what blessings I will accept and which I reject, I am actually exalting my own wisdom above His. I am saying that I know my needs better than He does. It is like saying, "You can do this and this for me, God, but I don't want You to do that." How much better and wiser to pray, "Enlarge my coast, Lord. Bless me. Do all that You want to do in my life."

Then Jabez prayed, "That Your hand would be with me."

It is vitally important to have the hand of God upon your life in all the things you do. And it is dangerous to undertake any project without it.

When Moses was leading the children of Israel into the Promised Land, he said to the Lord, "If Your Presence does not go with us, do not bring us up from here" (Exodus 33:15). In other words, "Lord, don't lead us anywhere You are not going."

If God goes with us, we can go anywhere—and we can go forth with assurance, comfort, and power.

Jabez's next petition was, "Keep me from evil...."

This is such an important prayer that Jesus included it as the last petition in the Lord's Prayer: "Deliver us from evil." The evil one is always trying to draw us into his snare.

It is easy to fall into the snare of the enemy and allow hatred or bitterness to begin to control our lives. Living a righteous life is difficult. In fact, it's not even possible by our own human energy. Only the power of the Spirit of God in us can enable us to live righteously.

Jabez continued, " … that I may not cause pain."

The primary result of evil is rarely grief. More often, it results in thrills and excitement. Evil often has the appearance of being prosperous. It looks like an easy way to make a quick buck. Of course, it isn't quite honest. An enticer might say to you, "But look at the profits you can make. And look at what you can do with the money that you get from the profits!"

The primary result of evil may be joy, excitement, pleasure, or possessions—but the end result of evil is always grief. You may not think so; sin may seem very exciting to you right now. But a wise man will always consider the final destination of the path he is taking.

Where is your path leading you? If it is a path of evil, my friend, it is leading you to grief. In Psalm 73, Asaph said he was envious of the foolish when he saw the prosperity of the wicked. It almost caused him to stumble in his walk and commitment to the Lord—until he considered the end result of their wickedness.

Like Jabez, we must be wise enough to ask God's help—that we would avoid evil and the pain it brings.

## GOD'S ANSWERS

What was the result of Jabez's prayer? The Bible said God granted him what he requested. Praise the Lord! Jabez asked God to bless him and God blessed him. He asked the Lord to enlarge his coast and the Lord enlarged his coast. Jabez asked God to keep His hand upon him, and God kept His hand on him. He asked God to keep him from evil, and the Lord kept him from evil.

How glorious to know that, "If we ask anything according to His will, He hears us. And if we know that He hears us, whatever we ask, we know that we have the petitions that we have asked of Him" (1 John 5:14–15).

I can pray with confidence for God to bless me, enlarge my coast, keep His hand upon me, and keep me from evil—for this is the will of God for my life.

Ask Him and you, too, shall receive.

## ADDITIONAL POINTERS ON PRAYER

We have looked at three great models for our prayer life: Jabez, the disciples, and Jesus. Before we move on to our next section, here are a few pointers to consider.

Pray with an attitude of watchfulness. In Colossians, Paul exhorts us to watch, which literally means to "stay awake." Sleepiness is one of the weaknesses of our flesh while we pray. When Jesus was in the garden of Gethsemane praying, He found His disciples asleep. He said, "What! Could you not watch with Me one hour?" (Matthew 26:40). God wants our minds to be sharp and alert when we talk to Him.

Pray with an attitude of gratitude. Paul also exhorts us to pray with thanksgiving (Colossians 4:2). Our prayers should always be coupled with thanksgiving. The psalms serve as an ideal example of this. David prayed for everything—for himself, for his friends, and for his enemies. He also filled the psalms with praises and thanksgiving unto God. They are as well-balanced with thanksgiving as with requests. Quite often—though not often enough—people come to me and say, "I don't have any problems to share with you. I just wanted to praise the Lord with you! The Lord has been so good to me. I want to tell you how He has been blessing my life." That is so exciting! I hear so many problems as a pastor that it is a great joy when someone says, "I just want to tell you the Lord is so good!" That is glorious!

Though God's shoulders are big enough to handle every problem we encounter, it is a shame when all we bring Him are problems. We ought to be praising and thanking Him more for who He is and for what He has already done for us. Certainly, personal petitions are necessary in our prayers. But if I only pray when I have some desperate need in my own life and only bring personal petitions to God, I am denying myself a fantastic blessing. Oh, that I would go to God with more praises and thanksgiving!

In the early days of the United States, the Puritans observed days of fasting and affliction. There was at least one day of fasting each month of the year. Then someone said, "Let's have a day of thanksgiving! We won't fast or afflict ourselves, but we'll have a feast to thank the Lord for all He has done." Thus, the tradition of thanksgiving began—not our American feast of Thanksgiving—but the habit of offering thanks to God on a regular basis.

Sometimes, a quick little prayer is appropriate in desperate circumstances—such as, "God, be merciful to me, a sinner," or "Jesus, take over my life." Just one short little prayer like that can be the difference between life and death, heaven or hell, darkness or light. Just cry out to the Lord from your heart: "Oh Lord, forgive me my sins and make me Your child." You could pray this even now. It could be a silent prayer. It could be one of those quick, responsive prayers from your heart to God. And God will hear and God will answer. Your life will be transformed by the power of the Spirit, and you will become a child of God.

As we noted earlier, relationship is essential in order for prayer to be effective. So if you do not have a relationship with God, there is only one prayer He is interested in hearing or will hear from you. It is the prayer that says, "God, be merciful to me, a sinner." Once you have established relationship, then as a child of God, any time you are in need, you can say one of those quick prayers and God will deliver you and strengthen you.

## HOW TO BE POWERFUL IN PRAYER

If you want to see a man of the Word and of prayer, take a look at Nehemiah. There is so much we can learn about prayer by examining the book that bears his name. The account of Nehemiah's prayers—and how God opened the doors for those prayers to be answered—is truly amazing.

In the Persian court of King Artaxerxes, Nehemiah held a very important position. He was the king's cupbearer which meant that among his other duties, he was to taste each cup of wine before handing it to the king. This was for the king's protection, in case someone thought to poison his wine in an effort to kill him. If the cupbearer didn't fall on the floor in convulsions, the king knew his wine was safe to drink.

This arrangement created a bond between the cupbearer and the king. The king depended upon him for his life. And the cupbearer demonstrated his devotion to the king through the tasting of his wine. In essence, every time he picked up that cup, he was saying, "I'm willing to die for the king."

Perhaps because of this closeness, the king took note one day that Nehemiah was not his usual self. "Why is your face sad, since you are not sick? This is nothing but sorrow of heart" (Nehemiah 2:2).

What the king didn't know was that Nehemiah had received a troubling report about his beloved Jerusalem. From the time the Chaldeans captured King Zedekiah in 586 BC, Jerusalem had been without walls. During that siege, the Chaldeans bound the king, put out his eyes, and carried him and the remaining people of Judah off to Babylon. They then burned the king's house and the houses of the people, tore down the walls surrounding the city, and set fire to the city gates.

The city had been without those walls for more than a hundred years. Nehemiah knew that. But when Nehemiah's kinsman, Hanani, and a group of his men traveled to Persia, Nehemiah heard about the condition of the people living within Jerusalem—news that caused him grief. "The walls are broken down and the city is in shambles. Because they have no defense, they are an easy prey. The people are demoralized. They are barely existing."

Nehemiah had inquired about those who had returned to Jerusalem from Babylonian captivity. Of all the Jews taken in 606 BC, only 42,000 left Babylon when given the chance. They returned to a city left in rubble—a city left defenseless. With the walls down, those within the city had no protection from their enemies. Jerusalem, a city the psalmist once called "beautiful in elevation, the joy of the whole earth" (Psalm 48:2), was no longer beautiful. It was a place of utter destruction, and its inhabitants were disheartened and distressed.

At the news, Nehemiah wept before the Lord. And then he fasted and prayed, confessing his sins and the sins of the people, and acknowledging God's righteous judgment against Jerusalem.

In his prayer, recorded in Nehemiah chapter 1, Nehemiah quoted God's Word back to Him. "Remember, I pray, the word that You commanded Your servant Moses, saying, 'If you are unfaithful, I will scatter you among the nations; but if you return to Me, and keep My commandments and do them, though some of you were cast out to the farthest part of the heavens, yet I will gather them from there, and bring them to the place which I have chosen as a dwelling for My name'" (Nehemiah 1:8-9).

Nehemiah then ended his prayer by asking, "Lord, give me mercy in the eyes of Artaxerxes the king."

Scripture tells us that Nehemiah learned of Jerusalem's destruction in the month of *Chislev* (December), in the year 446 BC, and began mourning, fasting, and praying. It wasn't until *Nisan* (March) that King Artaxerxes asked about his downcast demeanor. Because Nehemiah was a man of prayer, we can assume he spent those months praying about the burden he bore for Jerusalem.

When the king asked about his downcast countenance, Nehemiah—though "dreadfully afraid"—answered, "Why should my face not be sad, when the city, the place of my fathers' tombs, lies waste, and its gates burned with fire?"

The king then said, "What do you request?"

It was the moment for which Nehemiah had prayed and waited. His heart, I am sure, began to pound. It would have been easy to jump right in and lay his case before the king. But it is at this point that Nehemiah said, "So I prayed to the God of heaven. And I said to the king ... " (Nehemiah 2:1-5).

It is interesting that even though Nehemiah had been praying about this matter for about three months, he still felt compelled to offer this one last, quick little prayer to the Lord before he stepped into the opportunity.

We would do well to follow this example. When God's hand begins to move in a situation we have been praying over for a long time, it is important that we continue to cover the whole thing with prayer.

Nehemiah followed the correct order of things. He prayed first, and then he acted. Again, if we followed Nehemiah's example and always prayed before we acted, we wouldn't be as apt to act rashly or inappropriately.

We are not told exactly what Nehemiah prayed. It was just one of those prayers we often throw quickly toward God when we are taken by surprise, or when we are suddenly in a place of danger or opportunity. It's the kind of prayer you quickly cry out when you see the car come through the stop sign and you realize you are about to broadside it. As you apply the brakes, you say, "Oh Lord, help me." And then you close your eyes and wait for the crash. Then, when it doesn't happen, you open your eyes and find yourself in an odd position, perhaps, but you realize the Lord heard that quick little desperate prayer. It is the kind of prayer you utter when you are about to make an important decision, when you face a difficult task, or when you are overwhelmed or confused. Those are very appropriate times to offer a quick, "Lord, help me!"

Sometimes, though, we can't even articulate the words. Emergency prayers are often just prayers of the heart. It is comforting to know that when we can't even utter the words, God still hears the heart.

I am certain Nehemiah's prayer was a short prayer. There wasn't time to go into a long prayer before the Lord. The king probably wasn't even aware of his prayer. It was likely a pause so slight that the king didn't notice it—but God did.

It isn't the length of the prayer that makes it effective. Somehow we have developed in our minds the idea that the longer we pray, the more effective it is. Jesus said in Matthew 6:7 that the Pharisees had that misconception. He said that when they prayed, they used vain repetition because they thought that they would be heard for their many words. In other words, they thought that the longer they spent in prayer, the more effective it would be—even though they were praying vain repetitious prayers.

But the Bible tells us that, "The effective, fervent prayer of a righteous man avails much" (James 5:16). And Nehemiah's prayers had availed much. The door was now opened.

"What do you want?" the king asked. "What is your request?"

"Oh Lord, help!" Nehemiah prayed in his heart. Then he said:

"If it pleases the king, and if your servant has found favor in your sight, I ask that you send me to Judah, to the city of my fathers' tombs, that I may rebuild it."

The king asked Nehemiah how long his journey would take, and when he planned to return. They discussed the details, and then Nehemiah reported, "So it pleased the king to send me; and I set him a time" (Nehemiah 2:5-6).

God answered the persistent prayer—and the quick prayer—of Nehemiah. On the fourteenth day of March, in the year 445 BC, King Artaxerxes made a decree which authorized Nehemiah to return and rebuild the walls of the city of Jerusalem.

Prayer opened the door for Nehemiah to return to Jerusalem, and prayer sustained Nehemiah as he began rebuilding the wall. As so often happens, the moment Nehemiah and his men began their construction efforts, enemies gathered around to mock them. This is a favorite tool of Satan. He loves to use ridicule to discourage you in the work of God. "Just who do you think you are—

Billy Graham?" he asks. "Are you out to save the world?" None of us like to be ridiculed, so often this device works effectively to stop a person's ministry for God.

But Nehemiah handled their mockery correctly. Instead of battling the enemy himself, he prayed, "Lord, You have heard them. Wipe them out, Lord. Lead them into captivity" (Nehemiah 4:1-5).

Once again, Nehemiah provides a powerful example for us. It is better to commit the enemy into the hands of the Lord than to strike back yourself.

When Nehemiah's enemies realized their mockery wasn't stopping the builders, they plotted to attack at night and tear the wall down. The conspiracy came to Nehemiah's ears, and you can probably guess what his first reaction was. "We made our prayer to God, and because of them we set a watch against them day and night" (Nehemiah 4:9).

Prayer first, and then action. But don't overlook the action part of that sentence. After committing the situation to God, Nehemiah then ordered them to set a watch on the wall. Prayer should never be an excuse for idleness. For instance, if you have prayed for a job, you need then to go out and look for a job. God expects us to use the good sense He gave us. It is not a lack of faith to follow up your prayer with action—it is wisdom.

Be practical about your actions. If you have prayed and asked God to heal your poor eyesight, wait for the optometrist to retest you and say that you have been healed before you throw your eyeglasses in the trash. Prayer shouldn't lead you into reckless or careless action. It should actually create a diligence within you.

The Israelites prayed, and then they acted. They built the wall with a trowel in one hand and a sword in the other. The enemy saw that. With attack no longer an option, they plotted new ways to hinder Nehemiah's work.

But Nehemiah was already ahead of them. As he had done all through the situation, he committed the situation to prayer. "Oh, God," he prayed, "strengthen my hands" (Nehemiah 6:9).

The man of prayer brings everything to God—big things, little things, and everything in between. Though some act as though they believe God is too busy running the universe to bother with the trivial things in our lives, the man of prayer understands that our heavenly Father is conscious of the sparrow falling to the ground, and willing to help us in our every need (Luke 12:6-7).

Nehemiah was such a man. Because of his close fellowship with God, and because he prayed his way through every obstacle, the walls that had lain in rubble for over a hundred years were rebuilt in just fifty-two days. Not only that, a spiritual revival occurred among the people. While doing the physical work of God, Nehemiah and his men also did a spiritual work. The Israelites became so excited that their walls were rebuilt and they could again dwell securely in Jerusalem that they gathered together to worship the Lord. In the temple, Ezra the scribe brought out the law of God and read it to the people. This reading was accompanied by repentance and weeping before God. The hearts of the people were turned back to the Lord (Nehemiah 8–9).

Nehemiah's focus was on rebuilding the wall and securing Jerusalem for its inhabitants. He didn't know when he set out to begin his construction project that God was going to use his efforts for an even mightier purpose—the spiritual revival of His people. And whether Nehemiah realized this or not, God intended an even grander purpose out of this event. At the moment of Artaxerxes' decree, the countdown to the Messiah began.

Ninety-three years earlier, while Daniel was in Babylon and Belshazzar was still king, Daniel was in prayer when the angel Gabriel came to him and said, "From the going forth of the command to restore and build Jerusalem until Messiah the Prince, there shall be seven weeks and sixty-two weeks" (Daniel 9:25). That number, when multiplied equals 483 years. And so it was that 483 years after the decree of Artaxerxes, in the year 32 AD, Jesus came riding into Jerusalem on a donkey. What a glorious fulfillment of prophecy! This fact precludes any other person claiming to be the Messiah who did not show up in the year 32 AD, 483 years after this commandment to restore and rebuild.

Nehemiah, through prayer, was used by God at this critical moment in history. The door was opened—and Nehemiah went through it by the power of prayer. As you can see, one man living in prayer and fellowship with God can accomplish incredible results!

As I look around today, I see that we are living in a needy world. Conditions have never been so bad. Our world is morally corrupt and unable to help itself. What the world needs—desperately—is people who live in fellowship with God, who know the strength of God, and who are willing to pray for God's work to be done. We find a remarkable promise in 2 Chronicles 7:14 where the Lord said, "If My people who are called by My name will humble themselves, and pray and seek My face, and turn from their wicked ways, then I will hear from heaven, and will forgive their sin and heal their land."

Why not claim that promise? Why not be that man or woman of prayer for the sake of this poor, lost world—our nation, your city, your school, or perhaps even your own family?

## CHAPTER 6

# WHEN GOD WAITS

On occasion, it seems that God answers our prayers almost as quickly as we speak them. It happened that way for Eliezer, the servant Abraham sent to find a wife for Isaac. As he came to a certain well, Eliezer said, "Lord, let a young virgin come here to draw water, and when I say to her, 'Give me a drink,' let her answer, 'Not only will I give you a drink, but I'll also draw water for your camels.' Lord, let that woman be the one You have chosen as a bride for Isaac."

While the servant was yet praying in his heart, a young girl came to the well to draw water. He said to her, "Please let me drink a little water from your pitcher." She quickly let the water jug down from her head, gave him a drink, and then said, "I will draw water for your camels also, until they have finished drinking." And she drew water for the camels (Genesis 24:1–20).

This is one of those beautiful, instantaneous answers to prayer that always thrills us. No sooner do the prayers escape the heart than God is answering them. But I have discovered that God's timing often does not coincide with mine. Many times I have prayed for things and then waited … and waited … and waited … and waited for God to answer. Sometimes I waited so long I almost forgot that I had prayed in the first place. Just when I'd given up looking for an answer, the answer finally came.

We don't always know why God delays answering our prayers, but He does. And since Scripture is clear that His thoughts are higher than our thoughts, and His ways higher than our ways (Isaiah 55:9), we can be certain that God has good reasons for those times when He waits.

## MY SOLUTION

Whenever a problem comes up, one of the first things we usually do is try to figure out the solution on our own. Often we do "pillow planning." You know what that is. That is when you wake up at night because you are so worried about your problem that you can't stay asleep. Your mind is busy dealing with the situation, and you lay there tossing and turning, back and forth, trying to force out a solution. We begin to hypothesize, "If this happened, and if that happened, then it would all fall in place." There is no rest when you are pillow planning—just a lot of frantic thinking.

Once we have worked out the solution to our problem, we then set out to have a little show-and-tell time with God. We lay out the problem in great detail, as though He wasn't already aware of the situation and it is our responsibility to inform Him. Not only that, but we begin to counsel God on how He should deal with our problem. The Bible asks, "For who has known the mind of the LORD? Or who has become His counselor?" (Romans 11:34). The answer is: me. I have counseled God many times on just how He ought to handle things and what He should do in this situation. "Lord, this is what You need to do," as though God needed my counsel.

When we are in that show-and-tell, fix-it mode, our prayer then is not really a direct prayer, but a *direction* prayer, as we now begin to direct God in how to bring about the solution that we figured out on our own. "Now God," we say, "if You'll just help me win the sweepstakes, I'll be able to pay off all of these bills!"

There is a big difference between being direct and giving directions.

Perhaps you have found, as I have, that God often ignores our directions. He doesn't always listen to our solutions, and there is a good reason for this. It is because He has a much wiser solution than what we came up with. The problem is when God chooses to ignore our direction, we often get upset. We think God isn't listening to us. We think God doesn't care.

You bring a lot of frustration on yourself when you pray direction prayers, when, instead of asking God for help, you tell Him how He ought to do His business in your life. Sometimes at the root of our frustration we find impatience. *"What is the problem? Can't God see the wisdom of my solution?"* Often, on the heels of those thoughts come these: *"Is prayer really valid? Is it worthwhile?"*

I think of a man named Abraham, who waited a long time for God to answer his prayers for a son. Abraham was over a hundred years old before God answered that prayer. Since he likely married when he was about twenty, I imagine he waited for about eighty years for his prayer to be answered.

Why would God delay that long? We don't know. God doesn't tell us. Instead, He simply says, "Trust Me." Perhaps, through Abraham, God was giving mankind a classic example of "the just living by faith." For surely Abraham is a man who waited on God and lived his life *by faith*.

## GOD'S DESIRE

Sometimes God delays the answers to our prayers because He plans to do much more for us than we asked or prayed. He is waiting for us to come to a place of understanding before He answers the prayer. He knows that if He were to give the answer to us prematurely, before we are in harmony with His desires, we may abuse or misuse that which God gives to us. So sometimes God delays the answers, waiting for us to come around to His heart and to His purposes.

Delay is hard for us. I think of how uncomfortable delay was for Hannah, whose story is told in 1 Samuel. As was common in that time of history and in that culture, Elkanah, Hannah's husband, had two wives. Now I personally don't know why any man would think he had the capacity to satisfy two women. I find it difficult to keep *one* woman completely happy. That is a full-time job! But to take on two—that would present some real problems.

And it did. Because Elkanah obviously loved Hannah more than his other wife, Peninnah, it caused great rivalry and jealousy between the two women. Despite Elkanah's love, Hannah's culture considered her to be cursed—because she could not bear children.

Sons were so important in that culture that men could divorce their wives if they were unable to conceive. Men wanted a son to take their name and to carry on their household. So whenever a woman would go into labor, all of the neighbors would come with drinks and food and get ready for a party. The band would arrive and everyone would wait while the wife was in labor. If the midwife came out and said, "It's a girl," everyone would pack up and go home. But if she said, "It's a boy, everybody!" the band would start playing and everyone would have a great time celebrating.

Hannah was barren, but Peninnah was very prolific. Year after year, she gave Elkanah a new son or daughter, but Hannah was unable. Peninnah, being jealous of the fact that Elkanah loved Hannah more than he loved her, really rubbed it in. She would hold her infant and say, "Don't you wish you could have one of these? But you can't, because you are barren. Don't touch my child. Go have your own if you want to touch a child, but don't touch mine."

Peninnah, the Bible says, "provoked her severely" (1 Samuel 1:6). She really made life miserable for Hannah. So Hannah prayed continually, "God, give me a son so I could hold it up to her and say, 'Look what I've got!' I want a son. I've got to have a son. I've got to shut the mouth of this woman."

But nothing happened. Hannah remained barren. Things got so bad that Hannah couldn't eat, and she cried all the time.

Hannah didn't realize there were advantages to not having children. After all, when her husband, Elkanah, went every year up to Shiloh to worship God at the tabernacle, she got to go with him, while Peninnah had to stay home and take care of all her kids. Hannah had much more freedom than Peninnah. Yet, while traveling to Shiloh,

Hannah was so grieved over the fact that she didn't have any children that when they stopped by "McDavid's" to eat, she didn't order anything. Elkanah said to her, "Why aren't you eating? Why are you crying all the time? Am I not worth ten sons to you? I love you so much. You ought to be satisfied with me." But she wasn't. Hannah desperately wanted a son.

When they arrived at Shiloh, Hannah poured out her grief to God. So deeply did this thing trouble her that as she prayed, her face contorted and her mouth moved but she couldn't even utter words anymore. In her heart she prayed, "O LORD of hosts, if You will indeed look on the affliction of Your maidservant and remember me, and not forget Your maidservant, but will give Your maidservant a male child, then I will give him to the LORD all the days of his life, and no razor shall come upon his head" (1 Samuel 1:11).

Hannah's reference to a razor never touching his head indicated the vow of the Nazarite, which was one of complete and total consecration to God. She was promising God that if He would just give her that son, she would make sure he would be totally consecrated to God all the days of his life.

The high priest came by and saw her lying there, her mouth moving, but he couldn't hear anything. "Woman, quit your drinking!" he said. "That stuff will destroy you. Put your booze away."

Hannah looked up and said, "Sir, I am not drunk like you think. I have not had any wine or strong drink. But my soul is grieved and I have been pouring it out to God."

The priest, a little embarrassed that he had misjudged her, said, "Oh, go in peace and may God grant you your request."

Eli, the high priest, was a good man. But he had a great weakness in that he never disciplined his sons. As a result, his uncontrollable sons were rotten through and through. They had grown up now, and as Eli was quite old, his sons were in line to become high priest after him. Because they were sons of Levi, they stood to control the priesthood. But they were totally corrupt. They didn't revere the things of God at all. For example, by tradition when people would bring their offering they would boil the meat. It was customary for the priest to reach in the pot with a hook and grab hold of a chunk of meat. Whatever he grabbed was his. But these sons would approach the people bringing their sacrifices before the meat was boiled and say, "Don't boil that meat yet until we get our part. We don't want it boiled; we want it roasted. If you don't give it to us," they would say, "we'll take it by force." They abused the people and they abused their position as God's representatives. In fact, they so misrepresented God that they actually discouraged people from coming to Him.

A corrupted priesthood translates into a corrupted nation. This was a real low point in the history of the nation of Israel, both morally and spiritually. The corrupted priesthood had helped put the nation in a state of great moral decay, and Israel was ready to be destroyed by her enemies.

God wanted a man who would lead the nation back onto the path of righteousness, back to God, back to a place of strength. But though God looked all over Israel, He could not find such a man.

But God did find a woman. God closed up Hannah's womb and put her in an uncomfortable situation by opening the womb of the other wife, Peninnah. He even allowed Peninnah to torment Hannah, knowing it would bring her to a point of desperation.

In that state of desperation, Hannah prayed over and over and over, "God, I want a son. God, I *need* a son."

No answer. Why did God delay? God delayed because God wanted to give much more than a son. He wanted to give the nation a prophet, a priest, a judge who would lead the people back to God's path and who would save the nation from destruction. God wanted to give Hannah much more than what she was asking for, so He withheld her desire until finally she prayed, "Oh God, if You will but give me a son, I will give him back to You all the days of his life and he can be totally consecrated to You."

There is no better place to be than right in that place God desires for us; that place where He will give us so much more than we have asked Him for. And so God granted her prayer and gave her Samuel, that great prophet, that great priest, that great judge, who saved the nation by bringing them back into a right relationship with their God.

## GOD'S GIFTS

As we have discussed throughout this book, God is a giver. He is the giver of gifts, the giver of answers, the giver of help, the giver of all that we need. But the question is, *how* does God give? What is His attitude when He gives?

Let us first look at ourselves, and the ways we give. With man, we find that there are three basic types of givers. If our church were one that had a custom of setting the budget and then going out to the people for pledges to meet that budget and accomplish the goal for the year (and thank God it is not), the finance committee would start by putting together a psychological profile on all the members of the church. From those profiles, the board would determine just what kind of a giver each church member was. The board would then decide who would call on which members and press them for their pledge for the coming year.

These church boards know that with some people, you've got to put a little pressure on. So you get three or four prominent persons in the church to go to them—people they look up to and people by whom they want to be well thought. Let us say the board decides you are one who needs a little bit of pressure. These prominent people will head out one evening and knock on your door. Once you invite them in, they will begin talking to you about all the goals the church has for this next year, about how the church wants to build a new gymnasium and hopes to expand the church facilities. "We are going to put in a kitchen," they will say, "and we will have potlucks and your children will have a place to go in the evening. And everyone who gives over a thousand dollars will have their names listed on the board in the gymnasium, and people will be able to see those who contributed more than a thousand dollars. Incidentally, your neighbor next door has put in his contribution—well over a thousand dollars."

Finally, under all that pressure, you say, "Well, all right." You sign their pledge, even though you are reluctant to do so. They did what they came to do. Those committee members got your dollars, and that is all they really care about.

The second type of giver is the one who is ready to give, who wants to give, but who just needs to know what the need is. With this type of person, once the committee members begin to explain, "Now, the church really feels we need a new gymnasium—" you jump right in and say, "Oh, wonderful. I think that is a great idea. Let me have my pledge card."

The third type of giver is the one who looks around and says, "These kids don't have anything to do around here.

No wonder they are getting into mischief. We don't have recreational activities for them—no facilities, no recreational center. It would be tremendous if someone would develop a gymnasium and recreation center where the kids had a place to go at night." So they begin looking around and inquiring. "Do you have any plans for the future for recreation facilities?

The committee representatives say, "Yes, it just so happens this year we are planning to build a gymnasium."

"Oh, that's glorious. Let me get my checkbook." This type of giver has found someone who is in harmony with what they have a burden and a desire to do.

Now of these three basic types, into which category would you put God? A lot of people put Him in the first category. In their minds, prayer is a snow job. "God, if You'll help me to win the sweepstakes, I'll give You twenty percent. Not ten percent, Lord, but twenty percent. How can You lose on this one? You are going to do nothing but benefit. I'll even throw in regular attendance, if You'll just do this thing my way."

This kind of prayer is really a sales pitch to God. You think God is reluctant to answer your prayer, so you put the pressure on. But those who think God has to be caught in this way have misread Him completely.

Others think that prayer is information time. "Lord, You can't believe what I have been going through lately. Things really have been tough. The other day, the banker called me and told me my account was overdrawn." These people lay out the whole story for God, as though He didn't already know. But Jesus said, "Your Father knows the things you have need of before you ask Him" (Matthew 6:8). He doesn't need all the information—He already knows!

How does the Bible describe the giving nature of God? One day, Hanani, the seer came to King Asa and said, "For the eyes of the LORD run to and fro throughout the whole earth, to show Himself strong on behalf of those whose heart is loyal to Him" (2 Chronicles 16:9). What is God telling us through this verse? He is saying that He looks for people whose hearts are in harmony with His purposes—lives that are dedicated to those things He desires to do—in order that He might pour His resources through them. God is looking for places to work, lives through which He can work, lives through which He can invest His resources. All it takes is a heart that is completely towards Him, towards His purpose, and towards His plan.

In Hannah's situation, she finally came to the place of saying, "God, if You'll just give me a son, I will give him back to You all the days of his life, that he might be totally consecrated to You" (1 Samuel 1:11).

Now she is aligned with God's purpose, which is to find a man to deliver the nation, and God is ready to answer her prayer. God delayed in order to bring her around to that which He desired for the nation itself.

As we have seen, sometimes God waits because He is working something within you. But there is another reason why prayers are sometimes delayed. Sometimes, the work that needs to be done is not within you, it is within the spiritual realm. As we discussed earlier, the world is in the midst of heavy spiritual warfare. The forces of God and the forces of evil war against one another continually. And as prayer is a spiritual activity, our prayers have a weighty role in that battle. Satan fights against our prayers—and sometimes, delays the answers.

Take the case of Daniel. In chapter 10, we read that the rule of the Babylonian Empire was passing to the authority of the Persian Empire about the time Cyrus became king. In the third year of Cyrus' reign, Babylon was conquered and Daniel began living under Persian rule. He and some of his friends decided to go to the river to wait upon the Lord. After twenty-one days of fasting and praying, the angel of the Lord appeared to Daniel. He described the encounter this way: "I lifted my eyes and looked, and behold, a certain man clothed in linen, whose waist was girded with gold of Uphaz! His body was like beryl, his face like the appearance of lightning, his eyes like torches of fire, his arms and feet like burnished bronze in color, and the sound of his words like the voice of a multitude" (Daniel 10:5-6). Daniel's terrified friends fled, and he was left alone to face the angel. He lost all strength and fell to the ground, but the angel reached out and touched him, saying, "O

Daniel, man greatly beloved, understand the words that I speak to you, and stand upright, for I have now been sent to you." Daniel stood, but he trembled. The angel then said, "Do not fear, Daniel, for from the first day that you set your heart to understand, and to humble yourself before your God, your words were heard; and I have come because of your words. But the prince of the kingdom of Persia withstood me twenty-one days. And behold, Michael, one of the chief princes, came to help me, for I had been left alone there with the kings of Persia. Now I have come to make you understand what will happen to your people in the latter days, for the vision refers to many days yet to come" (Daniel 10:11-14).

Satan held back the answer for twenty-one days as he captured this emissary God had sent to Daniel with the answers to his prayers.

Spiritual warfare is a very real and great hindrance. Because of that warfare, and because prayer takes on the characteristic of a spiritual entity, many prayers must be repeated and persisted.

It is only natural to become impatient while we wait for the answers to our prayers. David knew that frustration. The psalmist sometimes asked, "Lord, why are You tarrying? Why do You wait so long? Answer me speedily." But we have to trust that when God waits, God has a reason. He is changing something in the spirit world, or He is changing something in you. Keep praying, align your will with His, and wait patiently. If your prayers agree with God's desires, you can be sure He will answer in due time.

If not—well, that is the subject of the next chapter.

## CHAPTER 7

# When God Says "No"—or Says Nothing at All

The great thrust behind prayer, the incentive for praying, is that things are wrought through prayer that would not have been wrought apart from prayer.

When we pray, a number of things may happen. God may say yes immediately. Or, as we saw in the last chapter, God may say yes after a delay. In this chapter, we will deal with two other outcomes: when God says "no" or when God says nothing at all.

"No" is not always a bad answer. We may initially feel disappointed or frustrated by a "no" answer, but in the long run, any answer God gives is the right answer. I have personally come to appreciate the "no" answers. I am grateful for many of the times when God heard my cry but didn't answer my prayer the way I offered it. I have often reflected on what big trouble I would be in today if God had said yes to every prayer I've tossed in His direction.

Back when I was in high school—this was way back in ancient history, when Santa Ana had only one high school—there was this black, three-window, '36 Ford Coupe for sale. This was the slickest car you ever saw—the heat risers were plugged, it had twin Smitty mufflers, big chrome hubcaps with a disk in them, twin spotlights, twin fog lights, twin antennas, custom upholstery—man, was that a beautiful car!

I coveted that car. Every day when I rode my bicycle past it, I would stop and walk around it, admiring the Buick emblems on the back. It looked sharp!

I started praying, "Lord, I would sure like to take kids to church ... if I only had a car. It is hard to take them on my bike, Lord. I really want that car. I *need* that car, Lord, so I can serve You! Please give me that car." I prayed and I prayed for that car. I wanted it desperately. I even fasted a couple of meals.

I could envision myself driving the kids to church each Sunday—that's true. But I also had another mental picture. I pictured myself driving past the high school at lunch hour when all the kids were out eating lunch. I imagined myself taking off in low gear and then just letting off the throttle and letting the pipe pop—so impressive—as I drove by. I could see all the girls turning their heads and seeing that beautiful, black, sharp car and saying, "Wow, I wish he would ask me out for a date and I could ride in that car."

"Lord, I *need* this car to take kids to church. Please, Lord."

God does answer prayer—not always as we ask, but always as is best for us. After a couple of months the car disappeared. Someone had bought it—breaking my heart. I went home and poured out my complaint to God. "Why don't You love me? You don't care about me. You don't answer prayer." My head was full of questions. If God doesn't answer prayer, then why do we pray? I went through the whole routine.

But as I look back on it now, I am thankful God didn't answer that prayer. That car could have just destroyed my entire future. God was wise, much wiser than I. He knew better. He knew how that car might have impacted my life. In His love, He was protecting me from myself. I didn't have enough sense, and so He had to overrule my desires and my decisions.

Through the years, God and I have developed an unwritten agreement: whenever I ask Him something that is not in keeping with His desire or purpose for me, He is just to ignore it. That is my agreement with God. You see, I really don't want anything that is contrary to God's plan and will for my life. I have learned that God's will for me is the best thing that could ever happen. I don't want anything that would hinder the work of God in my life.

"No" can be the best answer for us—and the best answer for those our lives affect. Look at Paul. He had an irritation—something he referred to as his "thorn in the flesh." Three times he asked God to remove it from him, but God denied that request. And that has proved to be a blessing to the rest of us, because it comforts us to see Paul's example. Despite the thorn, and despite the "no" answer from God, Paul continued to love, serve, and praise God. That helps us in dealing with our own thorns.

God used that thorn to bless and comfort us, and He used it to humble Paul. You see, Paul had been given an abundance of visions—revelations—and without that thorn in his flesh, Paul may have become prideful. As he put it, "And lest I should be exalted above measure by the abundance of the revelations, a thorn in the flesh was given to me, a messenger of Satan to buffet me, lest I be exalted above measure" (2 Corinthians 12:7). Paul was so aware of the temptation to be "exalted above measure" that he stated it twice in the same sentence. He then added, "Therefore I take pleasure in infirmities, in reproaches, in needs, in persecutions, in distresses, for Christ's sake. For when I am weak, then I am strong" (2 Corinthians 12:10). Paul actually learned to rejoice over that rotten thorn, because he experienced the mighty power of God as a result of it.

I am glad God said no to Paul. And I am so blessed that He said no to Jesus there in the garden of Gethsemane when Jesus asked that the cup pass from Him. God said no to that request, and Jesus obeyed and drank the cup. Why? Because God wanted to bring salvation to each of us.

It must be noted that after making His request, Jesus added what is so important to every prayer: "Nevertheless not My will, but Yours, be done" (Luke 22:42). That is the key. "Lord, here is what I want. Here is my desire. Nevertheless not my will, but Yours, be done." You can't improve on that! For the real purpose of prayer is never to get my will done, but God's.

So sometimes God says no because He is working out a larger purpose. And then there are those situations where a "no" answer comes as a consequence to one of our choices. Even then, God may be working good through that denial.

For instance, Moses prayed that God would allow him to go into the Promised Land. But God said, "No, Moses. For the sake of the people you can't go into the land. You misrepresented Me before those people. Now they must learn the lesson of obedience." Moses—that mighty, spiritual giant who communed face-to-face with God—was denied permission to go into the Promised Land (Numbers 20:7–12).

Now consider this. Throughout the centuries, from that time until now, parents have told their children the story of Moses, the man of God, who was used by God to deliver the children of Israel from Egypt and bring them to their own land. They tell of the many amazing deeds of Moses—about how he went up into the mountain and received the law of God in the midst of the fire and rolling thunder, and about the way his face shone so that he had to cover himself with a veil, and about the moment when he stretched forth the rod and the Red Sea parted. And then with whispered tones they say to their children, "But Moses could not go into the land because he disobeyed God."

In order to teach the future generations of the nation of Israel the lesson of the importance of complete obedience, God said "no" to Moses' prayer.

Aside from those situations when our disobedience denies us a blessing, what prompts God to say no? And what about those times when our prayers go up but seem to bring down nothing at all? Over the years, I have discovered that when our prayers are not answered, or when God says no, it is usually for one of four reasons.

## FOUR REASONS FOR A "NO" ANSWER—OR NO ANSWER AT ALL

### 1. YOU HAVE FAILED TO PRAY

It must be asked: Have you really prayed about the situation you are in? Have you asked God for the help you need?

Sometimes we *think* we have prayed about something, because it is constantly on our minds and we are mumbling to ourselves about it and talking to everybody else about it. But until you stop to pray, you haven't really talked to God about it yet. James gives us the first reason for unanswered prayer: "You do not have because you do not ask" (James 4:2). Often the problem is just that simple. I haven't received an answer because I haven't asked.

A woman once approached the captain of an ocean liner crossing the Atlantic in a severe storm. As she looked at the waves breaking over the deck, she said, "Oh, Captain—are we going to make it?"

"Woman," the captain answered, "we just have to trust the Lord."

"Oh my!" the woman said. "I didn't know it was that serious."

We act as if we have reached the end when we come to that place where we have to trust the Lord. It is as if we think, "Well, we have tried everything else. Every other option is gone. Let's see—what's left ...? Oh! Prayer." It is as if God is a last resort rather than a first resort.

Oh, the mess we make of things when we act before we have sought God through prayer. Sometimes we are our own worst enemy—times when we move ahead or make a decision without seeking God, simply because the action or the choice seems so obvious. "What do you mean, pray? Anybody can see what you should do in this situation."

Joshua discovered what a mistake that could be. While leading the children of Israel into the Promised Land, Joshua and the people had conquered Jericho, Bethel, and Ai. As they were about to move into the land, they were approached by a group of men with ragged clothes, tattered shoes, and moldy bread.

The strangers said, "From a very far country your servants have come, because of the name of the LORD your God; for we have heard of His fame, and all that He did in Egypt, and all that He did to the two kings of the Amorites who were beyond the Jordan—to Sihon king of Heshbon, and Og king of Bashan, who was at Ashtaroth. Therefore our elders and all the inhabitants of our country spoke to us, saying, 'Take provisions with you for the journey, and go to meet them, and say to them, "We are your servants; now therefore, make a covenant with us."' This bread of ours we took hot for our provision from our houses on the day we departed to come to you. But now look, it is dry and moldy. And these wineskins which we filled were new, and see, they are torn; and these our garments and our sandals have become old because of the very long journey." The record goes on to say, "Then the men of Israel took some of their provisions; but they did not ask counsel of the LORD" (Joshua 9:9-14).

Joshua signed the treaty. In doing so, he was saying, "We don't have to ask God about this. Look at the moldy bread. Look at the holes in those fellows' shoes. We don't have to seek God on this one."

Joshua, the children of Israel, and the strangers traveled on together. As they came to the next city—the city of Gibeon—Joshua began to deploy the troops to attack. But the strangers stopped them.

"Oh no, you can't attack this city!" the men said.

"What do you mean?" Joshua said, "It is in our way and we are going to conquer it. Besides, you said you came from very far away."

"No!" the men protested. "This is our city. This is where we have come from."

And Joshua knew, in that minute, he had been tricked.

In the hymn, "What a Friend We Have in Jesus," one verse declares, "Oh, what needless pain we bear; all because we do not carry everything to God in prayer."

"You do not have because you do not ask." Make sure you haven't forged ahead without first seeking the Lord. You will save yourself a lot of trouble and a lot of heartache.

## 2. UNCONFESSED SIN HAS BROKEN THE CONNECTION

Prayer is connection with God. And connections can be broken.

Think for a minute about the telephone. What an interesting invention. I can pick up the phone, dial a number, and instantly be connected with a friend in another town or even another country. But what if someone has cut the phone wire? I can still dial the number and talk into the telephone. I can imagine myself speaking to my friend and talk convincingly about all the things we might do if he would come for a visit. But no matter how persuasively I speak, my speaking is in vain, because there is no connection between us.

Sometimes people offer up very convincing prayers, but the connection between them and God has been broken. They think, "Well, I know I'm not living as I should, but that doesn't matter because I still pray." But those prayers are meaningless because there is no connection.

What are some of the things that can break the connection between God and us?

The first connection breaker is sin. As David said in Psalm 66:18, "If I regard iniquity in my heart, the Lord will not hear." And in Isaiah 59:1-2, the prophet said, "Behold, the LORD's hand is not shortened, that it cannot save; nor His ear heavy, that it cannot hear. But your iniquities have separated you from your God; and your sins have hidden His face from you, so that He will not hear."

When our connection with God is broken, the problem is not with God. The problem is with us. We have broken the connection through sin, because sin breaks the relationship between God and us. It is not possible to have deep communion with God if we are harboring sin in our life.

Is there a sin issue in your life right now? Is there something you know God has been dealing with you about, but you have refused to let it go? It is important for you to realize that by not giving it over to the Lord, you are regarding iniquity in your heart. That means your connection with God will be broken and your prayers will be hindered.

### 3. YOU ASK WITH WRONG MOTIVES

Another issue that breaks our connection with God is when we pray with wrong motives. James explains it this way: "You ask and do not receive, because you ask amiss, that you may spend it on your pleasures" (James 4:3). In other words, you ask for the things you want without considering what God wants. You ask for things that fulfill your own lust for pleasure.

This can be very subtle—so subtle, in fact, that we are often unaware ourselves that we are praying with a selfish motive. I'm embarrassed to admit this, but I recall such a time in my own life. In the early years of my ministry, the second pastorate I had was a small church in Tucson, Arizona that provided me with a salary of $25 per week. As you can imagine, it was hard to make ends meet on just $25 a week. I remember going out into the desert near the Sahuarita Range and spending days out there fasting and praying that God would bless our little church. I would ask Him to send more families into our church so we could have a real impact on the city of Tucson. Did I want that? Did I want people to get saved and our community to be impacted? Of course. But I had another motive, a selfish motive. In my heart I was thinking, "Just a few more families would mean better offerings, and that might mean they could raise my salary some, and that would make things so much easier." And that would fuel my prayers. "Oh, Lord! Send revival! Send new families to our church!"

Oh, but the heart is deceitful. Sometimes we don't even realize how impure our motives are.

Here is another example. Let us say a Christian wife is praying for her unbelieving husband. "Lord, help him to accept Jesus Christ. Help him to start coming to church with me and to have a desire to serve You." There is nothing wrong with that prayer; right? But let us say that deep down, what she is thinking is, "I'm tired of going to church alone and having people look at me with pity. I'm tired of seeing couples there together while I sit alone week after week. I wish my husband would come with me. If he became a Christian, he might even be a little more considerate around the house. We would probably fight less and he would probably treat me better. Oh, Lord—save him. Please save my husband."

Motives have a way of exposing themselves. Say the husband does come to Christ. Say he does begin to come to church and get involved in ministry. One day, after he has been serving for awhile, he comes home and says, "You know, honey, the Lord has really been speaking to my heart. I believe He is calling me into ministry, so I have decided to give up my career."

"What?" the wife exclaims. This was not in the plan. "Ministry? How in the world are we going to survive?"

"Well," he begins, "we will have to sell our house—"

"Whoa!"

And the motive is revealed. That prayer for her husband's salvation was a convenient prayer. But when the heat is on, the truth becomes apparent.

David said, "Search me, O God, and know my heart; try me, and know my anxieties; and see if there is any wicked way in me" (Psalm 139:23-24). That is a good prayer. We need God to search our hearts, because they are deceitful and desperately wicked, and we don't always know it. We hear our own prayers and think, "Oh my, that is wonderful. I'm asking for good, legitimate things." But the subtle truth is, behind those beautiful prayers lurk selfish motives.

## 4. YOU HAVE AN UNFORGIVING SPIRIT

The fourth thing that can break your connection with God is an unforgiving spirit. When Jesus spoke of prayer, He often tied it together with the need for forgiveness. "Forgive us our debts, as we forgive our debtors" (Matthew 6:12). At the conclusion of His prayer, Jesus then stopped and emphasized this petition on forgiveness, saying, "But if you do not forgive men their trespasses, neither will your Father forgive your trespasses" (Matthew 6:15).

You know, the shortest distance between two points is not always a straight line. Jesus said, "If you bring your gift to the altar, and there remember that your brother has something against you, leave your gift there before the altar, and go your way. First, be reconciled to your brother, and then come and offer your gift" (Matthew 5:23-24). In other words, the shortest distance between you and God may not be a direct path—it might be a path that leads by an offended brother's home. Get things right with your brother. Forgive. And then come and offer your gift.

We are sometimes stingy with our forgiveness. But Jesus addressed this when Peter, probably trying to impress Him with his suggestion, asked, "Lord, how often shall my brother sin against me, and I forgive him? Up to seven times?" I think Peter stretched the number of times he thought he could forgive a person. I think when he asked this, in the back of his mind Peter thought, *"Aren't I growing in grace and understanding, Lord? Aren't You proud of me?"* So it probably came as a shock when Jesus answered, "I do not say to you, up to seven times, but up to seventy times seven" (Matthew 18:21-22).

Four hundred and ninety times? That is a lot of forgiveness. I am sure Jesus figured Peter would lose count by the time he got that far. By then, hopefully, he would realize that forgiveness is not a matter of mathematics—it is a matter of the spirit.

While on the way to church recently, I began thinking of all the things God has forgiven me for, and all the grace He has extended to me. I was aware of just how undeserving I am of that forgiveness and grace. And as I meditated on God's goodness, two things happened. One was that I felt a need to thank Him and worship Him. The other was that I became aware all over again of how necessary it is for us to forgive one another. In light of how much God has forgiven us, who are we to hold on to petty grievances? Who are we to say, "I'll never forgive so-and-so for such-and-such"?

Inevitably, when the discussion of forgiveness arises, someone says, "Yes, but you don't know what this person did to me. If you knew how horrible he was to me, you would understand that I simply cannot forgive him."

I know it can be hard. People say things to you, or do things to you, or take advantage of you, and you think, "There is no possible way I can forgive this." I have experienced that myself. But I know I must forgive. I don't want to break the connection between God and me. I don't want to choke off the blessings He wants to send upon my life. And so when I come up against these issues where forgiveness is necessary but seems impossible, I begin by praying: "God, help me. Help me to forgive. Work in my heart, Lord. I can't do it in and of myself; it's just not in me. But You can." And He does. God never asks us to do a thing without giving us the strength to obey. If I am willing to forgive, God will give me the capacity to forgive.

Remember that to withhold forgiveness from another person really hurts you more than it hurts them. Is it worth it to you to hang on to unforgivingness if you know that you are robbing yourself of blessing and cutting off the connection between God and yourself?

## TAKE INVENTORY

So there is a checklist for you. If it seems that God has not been answering your prayers, or has been saying no, ask yourself a few questions. Is there sin in your life? Are there issues God has been dealing with you about? Are you praying with the right motive? Is there a brother or sister you need to forgive? Get rid of those hindrances, those things that are breaking your connection with God, and see what happens. You will find a new power in your prayers.

CHAPTER 8

# Prayerlessness

Do you realize that God wants to do great things for you—and great things *in* you? It is true. As you walk with the Lord, God will lift you up to the highest level you allow Him, and He will do His best for you—on that level. Unfortunately, so many times we limit what God wants to do in our lives by insisting on our own way instead of yielding to His way. God would do so much *more* for us! But often we are too busy insisting, "This is the way I want it, God!" If you reject God's divine plan and demand your own way, you will slip from God's best for your life—the thing He wants to do in and for you—to second best, or third best—or worse.

Such was the case with Israel. Though once a theocracy, a nation governed by God, the moment came in Israel's history when the people no longer wanted God to rule over them. Instead, wanting to be like all the other nations, they demanded a king. This proved to be a time of national disaster as Israel deteriorated from a theocracy to a monarchy.

God let Israel have its own way. He accommodated the demands of the people and commanded Samuel to anoint Saul as king. Notice that God did not announce, "I'm through with you!" and wipe out the Israelites. They were still God's people. However, God wanted the Israelites to know He was displeased with their decision. Through Samuel, He told them He was going to send rain on their wheat fields that were ready to be harvested. And He did so. The rain came and the people grew fearful. They cried out to the Lord, "We have sinned!" And they begged Samuel, their prophet, "Pray for your servants to the LORD your God, that we may not die; for we have added to our sins the evil of asking a king for ourselves" (1 Samuel 12:16, 19).

Samuel answered, "Do not fear. You have done all this wickedness; yet do not turn aside from following the LORD, but serve the LORD with all your heart ... For the LORD will not forsake His people, for His great name's sake, because it has pleased the LORD to make you His people." Then he said these amazing words: "Moreover, as for me, far be it from me that I should sin against the LORD in ceasing to pray for you" (1 Samuel 12:20, 22–23).

According to this passage, it is actually a sin *not to pray*. How many times are we guilty of the sin of prayerlessness?

Think of what a reproach it is to God when you do not pray. The Creator of the universe has invited you to fellowship with Him. He has invited you to enter into His presence to share any problems or needs you might have. Yet, so often we ignore this invitation.

Imagine finding in your mailbox a letter bearing the engraved, full-color, embossed seal of the President of the United States. You tear open the letter and find a formal invitation to the White House with all expenses paid. What would you do? Would you toss it away? No. Whether you agree with him or not, the President is an important person. Would you fail to respond to his invitation? Of course not.

If you respond to a human being's invitation with graciousness, think of the reproach it is when you refuse the invitation of God.

You may say, "I just don't have time to pray." But let me ask you this: Do you have time to watch television? We make time to do the things we really want to do. If we don't make time to pray, God must assume that we really don't want to fellowship with Him. And that is a correct assumption.

Our flesh rebels against prayer because it is an exercise of the spirit. That is why we get so tired the minute we start to pray. We say, "I'm too sleepy to pray right now, Lord." The flesh is rebelling against the spiritual exercise of prayer.

Remember the battle that is constantly waging. The spirit and flesh are always warring against each other. So whenever we enter into spiritual exercise, the flesh rebels against it. We find any excuse possible. "I'm too upset to pray," or "I'm too weak to pray."

Besides being a reproach to God, prayerlessness actually hinders the work of God in our lives.

You may ask, "Isn't God sovereign? Can't He do whatever He wants to do? Doesn't He rule over the entire universe? Aren't His purposes going to be accomplished no matter what? How can prayerlessness hinder the work of God?"

It is absolutely true that God is sovereign. But it is also true that God has created us as free moral agents. We have the capacity to choose and act freely, and God respects your free moral agency. God wants to do many things in and through you, but He will not coerce His will or His desires upon your life. He has given you the ability to choose, and He honors your choice.

Does that mean that prayerlessness limits God's work on the earth? No. Prayerlessness will hinder the work God wants to do in *your* life, because He will not override your own will, but His purposes for the earth are not limited by our weakness or our inactivity.

God has a plan for this earth, and He will bring that plan to fruition. The fact is God could work in any way He wants. Angels do His bidding. Creation obeys His every word. God is completely sovereign, completely powerful.

He doesn't need our help, but He allows us to help Him. What an incredible gift!

Because God chooses to work through human instruments, sometimes people say things like, "If you fail to help in the purposes of God, the program of God is going to fail—and you will be responsible! You will have to stand before God and answer for that failure!" Not true. Even if we fail, God isn't going to fail. God will accomplish His purpose one way or another.

When the survival of the Jewish race was being threatened by a cruel edict, Mordecai told Esther, "If you remain completely silent at this time, relief and deliverance will arise for the Jews from another place, but you and your father's house will perish" (Esther 4:14). He was warning her that when Haman's plan went into action and the Jews were wiped out, she would not escape the edict, even though she was in the palace.

Likewise, if you fail to do God's will, deliverance will come from another quarter. You will lose the blessing and the reward of being a co-laborer with God, but God's program and purpose will not fail. By choosing to use you to do His will, God is giving you the blessed opportunity of knowing the joy of working together with Him. Then, as results begin to take place, He rewards you as though you did the work! When you get to heaven you will be rewarded for those accomplishments, even though it was God who did the whole thing!

God commands us to pray. Therefore, failure to pray does not just rob us of the blessing of working together with God; it is also an act of disobedience against God. The Bible says, "Pray without ceasing" (1 Thessalonians 5:17) and, "Men always ought to pray and not lose heart" (Luke 18:1). Failure to pray is a sin because I am disobeying the actual command of God.

We need to pray for one another. I am convinced that as a pastor, I sin if I fail to pray for my flock. The Scripture says, "Pray one for another" (James 5:16). "Bear one another's burdens, and so fulfill the law of Christ" (Galatians 6:2).

As long as we are on the subject of praying for one another, I would like to remind you that Paul also exhorts us to pray for ministers (Colossians 4:3). May God help the ministers. Often, people place ministers on a pedestal and make us into something we are not. We are all too human. I wish I were more of a saint, but I am not!

The fact is, ministers have problems just like everybody else. We go through the same trials, perhaps to an even greater degree than most other Christians. Many times we are under heavier attacks by Satan because of our position of spiritual authority and leadership.

Someone once asked Spurgeon about his success. He answered, "My people pray for me." And that is what Paul admonished: "Pray for us." He wanted prayer that God would open a "door for the Word." At the point Paul wrote that letter, he was in prison. You would think he would ask them to pray for liberty. You would think he would have said, "Pray that God will open the door of the prison and get me out of this place!" Instead Paul prayed that God would open the door of opportunity to freely speak the Word.

I am not afraid to say that I covet your prayers. If you are willing, please pray that God will continually fill me with His Spirit, that I would have His power. Pray that God will help me to speak those things that please Him, not necessarily those things that please and excite the people. Pray that I will be a faithful minister, speaking forth the mysteries of Christ, demonstrating His love to the people, setting an example before the flock, and walking humbly before God as He would have me to do.

Pray for your ministers. We covet your prayers. And in turn, we will pray for you.

## CAUSES OF PRAYERLESSNESS

Numerous things can cause prayerlessness—laziness, complacency, perhaps even fear. But usually prayerlessness stems from one of four causes:

### 1. IMPATIENCE

Sometimes our prayerlessness is the result of impatience. Maybe we begin praying about a certain problem in another person's life. But when the problem doesn't immediately go away, we become discouraged and we quit praying. Or we become upset with other people's failures, even though we may have those same faults in our own lives. Our sins always look horrible when someone else is committing them.

Samuel had prayed that God would change the people's minds so they would no longer insist on a king. Samuel wanted God to rule and reign over the nation. But after all his prayers, the children of Israel still insisted on a king. Samuel easily could have become disgusted and said, "I'm not going to pray for those stubborn, stiff-necked people anymore! They have what they asked for. Let them reap the consequences." But he didn't stop praying. Instead, he said to them, "Moreover, as for me, far be it from me that I should sin against the LORD in ceasing to pray for you; but I will teach you the good and the right way" (1 Samuel 12:23).

## 2. DEMANDS

In this society we have allowed ourselves to become far busier than God originally intended. When the Lord first created our bodies He intended for man to live at a much easier, much more relaxed pace than we live now. Today, our lifestyle and our society work against us finding time to be alone with the Lord.

People seldom ignore work in order to spend time with God, but they think nothing of ignoring God so they can spend more time working. We justify that attitude by saying, "I have a mortgage to pay. I have to work that second job," or "Johnny needs braces. Work comes first." So many demands on our time, our attention, our energy. What we don't stop to realize is that we put a lot of those demands on ourselves, and fulfilling them comes at a great price. Not only does it add stress to our lives, it costs us time with the Lord.

## 3. DISTRACTIONS

Have you noticed how difficult it is to find an undisturbed place to pray? It is getting harder and harder to find a quiet place to be alone with the Lord. This world is noisy, congested, and overcrowded—and becoming more so by the day. Satan uses that noise and interruption to try to hinder your time with the Lord.

Assuming you find a quiet place to meet with God, what happens then? Distraction happens. Earlier we talked about the fact that so often, the moment we finally kneel down to pray, the phone rings. Or someone knocks at the door. Or the children come running in yelling and screaming and carrying on. Or you begin to think of everything you need to buy at the grocery store, or that phone call that you really need to return.

It doesn't take much at all to pull our attention away from God, and Satan knows it.

## 4. DROWSINESS

If impatience doesn't fizzle our prayer life, and demands

don't stop us from spending time with God, and distractions don't hinder our quiet time, drowsiness will do it.

Part of the problem with being so busy all the time is that we are tired. No one gets enough sleep anymore. So whenever we do find a free moment, our bodies cry out for rest. Watch what happens when, after a busy, hectic day, you kneel down beside your bed, put your head in your arms, and start to pray. Your body recognizes that position as a great position for sleep, and before you know it, you have dozed off—right in the middle of a prayer. After awhile your legs and knees begin to ache, and the discomfort wakes you up. You suddenly realize, "I have been sleeping on the job!"

A more dangerous position is lying on the bed and praying with your head on the pillow. Now, I must confess here that I do go to sleep every night talking to the Lord. I enjoy communing with the Lord until I am asleep. But it is necessary to have time during the day when you speak to God with a mind that is active and alert.

## SOLUTIONS

So what can we do to overcome our problem of prayerlessness? I have a few practical suggestions.

### 1. STAY THE COURSE

Don't give up. Don't let impatience steal the victory God wants to give you. Tell yourself that every prayer you offer up on behalf of another person wears down the enemy just a little bit more. When you begin to think, *"What's the use?"* stop that thought in its track and ask God for renewed strength for your task. Pray faithfully—no matter how long it takes.

## 2. MAKE TIME

Everyone has demands on their time. The solution is to put God at the top of your list and discipline yourself to take time for prayer. You will never *find* time to pray. You must *make* time.

Life is made up of priorities. Since you can never do all that you want to do, you must choose to sacrifice the less important things for the more important ones. A wise man makes good use of his time and keeps his priorities in proper perspective.

Prayer is the most important activity you could ever engage in. It should be at the top of your priority list of things to do. Even if you have to skip your time to eat or read the newspaper, you need to make time for prayer.

## 3. FIGHT THE DISTRACTIONS

It may take some doing to find a quiet, private place to meet with God, but it is worth the effort. Be creative. Many times I go for a walk or take a drive to get alone with the Lord. I also wake up much earlier than the rest of my family, so I have the house to myself. Prayer is more important to me than my sleep, and the phone rings very seldom in the early morning, so there is less chance of being interrupted.

To keep my mind from wandering, I usually vocalize my prayers. It's true that God knows what is in my heart, but when I try to pray out of my heart my mind often wanders. For a moment I am thinking, *"Lord, please take care of this and that. Thank You for blessing us with ... "* but pretty soon, my mind takes a side journey and I start thinking about the surf conditions in Hawaii, and how that next set of waves looks like a beauty— "Oops! Sorry, Lord." When I vocalize my prayer, though, I have to think about what I am saying. That causes me to concentrate on my conversation with the Lord.

I have found it is best for me to pray while sitting in a chair. I don't even close my eyes—it's way too dangerous. As a child, I was told that if I didn't close my eyes, the Lord wouldn't hear me. A pastor once mentioned that when he was playing basketball in junior high, the team decided to pray before the game. One of the kids said, "All right, everybody close your eyes or we'll lose." As they were praying, he peeked to see if they were all closing their eyes. When the team lost, he figured it was his fault. He felt guilty over that game for years!

However, in the Scriptures we are told to pray without ceasing (1 Thessalonians 5:17), which certainly indicates that prayer is not a position of the body. If I have to kneel down to pray, praying without ceasing would mean that I would never get off my knees.

Likewise, God does not expect us to always pray with our eyes closed, because prayer without ceasing would mean that I would never again open my eyes! Whether my eyes are open or closed, God hears all my prayers just the same.

## 4. FIGHT THE DROWSINESS

I have found that a good solution to drowsiness while praying is walking. If I am walking, I can't fall asleep. Sometimes I even walk back and forth in a room. Other times I go for a walk in a field or in the yard and talk to God. Some of my most fruitful and blessed prayer times have been during walks.

Another practical suggestion is this: get more sleep. Try shutting off the TV and getting eight hours of sleep. You will work better, feel better, and definitely be less likely to nod off during your prayer time. Give it a try.

## 5. BE REAL WITH GOD

Prayer will become a more regular part of your life if you see it for what it is—a conversation with the God who loves you. So often, people try to fancy up their prayer life with a lot of King James English and wild tones and shouting. Maybe they heard someone else pray and decided to incorporate all that person's little idiosyncrasies into their own prayers. They acquire a peculiar *prayer voice* where they sustain their words and add a touch of vibrato to punch up the words. "Oooh, God." I think they think that is the way to impress God. But that doesn't impress Him. Would it impress you if your child came up to you and said, in an unnatural voice, "Oooh, dear faaather!" I doubt it.

Just be real with God. It is easy—and I imagine very tempting—to set aside prayer when it is a big, dramatic production every time you kneel down to pray. That is exhausting. After awhile, I would think you would lose the heart to keep at it.

When I pray, I talk to God just like I would talk to my closest friend. God knows the real me. I have never found the need to use a "prayer tone." I tell Him all my problems, doubts, and questions—and I do it in a very matter-of-fact way. I try to be as honest with Him as I can. I might as well, because He knows if I am not! If I try to gloss over something, the only one who is getting fooled is me. God isn't fooled.

I may say, "Lord, You know I don't really have the depth of love for this fellow that I should have." This is an attempt to hide the truth and mask my true feelings. I might as well tell Him, "God, I can't stand him. I would like to punch him in the nose every time I see him!" Be honest—and then repent!

Talking to God in a conversational way means that I talk,

but I must listen, too. After all, God wants to speak to me. I find such joy and blessings as I come into this communion and fellowship with the One who created me.

May God forgive us our sin of prayerlessness. May God help us to pray fervently—and regularly. And as we become people of prayer, may we see the mighty work of God accomplished in this desperate world through our prayers.

# THE PROMISES

## CHAPTER 9

# Privileges and Promises

To fully appreciate prayer, we need to understand its definition, its use, and the results. In Section I, we dealt with the "what" of prayer—its definition. In Section II, we looked at the "how" of prayer—its use. Now here, in Section III, we will look at the "why" of prayer—results in the life of the believer.

## THE SCOPE OF PRAYER

The Christian has one source of power in his life: the Holy Spirit. Before Jesus ascended, He told His disciples, "You shall receive power when the Holy Spirit has come upon you" (Acts 1:8).

The Holy Spirit is the source of power in your life; however, your greatest outlet of spiritual power is prayer. I can do more for God through prayer than I can through any other means, including service. Prayer binds the strong man of the house, whereas service is going in and taking the spoil. Until you have prayed, there is no use in trying to do anything more. After you pray, you can then take action—but prayer must be first. Your service to God, though important, is limited to one place. Prayer, however, is limitless in its scope. Prayer can reach around the world.

Through prayer I can spend one-half hour of my life in South America doing work for the kingdom of God by strengthening the hands of the missionaries, and then I can go to Mexico and spend time with my friends who are ministering there. I can help them by praying for the effectiveness of the tracts they distribute and the words they speak. Then I can move into China and pray for the church there. I can touch a world for God through prayer, right from my own closet.

## THE PRIVILEGE OF PRAYER

Everyone engages in prayer at one time or another. When crisis looms, even that person who insists, "I don't believe in God," cries out, "Oh God, help me!" We are all acquainted with prayer to some extent or another.

I have to repeat it, because we seem numbed to its truth: Prayer is a glorious privilege. It is a gift God has made available to even the weakest of His children—and one of the greatest blessings God has given to man. It amazes me that I can come into the presence of God, the Creator of this universe, and talk with Him. And what is even more amazing—He always listens to me!

I am also amazed that God's door is always open. He has given me the privilege of talking with Him at any time. I don't have to make an appointment or call in advance. I can come at any hour, for any need, and open my heart before Him. And God not only listens, He has also promised to help me, to guide me, and to provide for my every need.

I imagine one of the great mysteries among the angels in heaven is that man has been given this glorious privilege of prayer, yet he takes such little advantage of it and treats it in such a peculiar way.

Many people treat prayer as a religious work that they must do. After they have prayed for a time, they expect a merit badge for their work. "After all, I prayed a whole hour"—as if they should be *rewarded* for talking to God.

Many people determine to pray an hour a day because it seems like an honorable thing to do. They start the hour of prayer by lifting up every request imaginable. When ten minutes have passed and they have run out of things to say, they start over again—and again. Finally, they get through that long hour and they feel good. "Praise the Lord!" they say. "I have spent a whole hour praying." And they go their way convinced they have fulfilled their obligation.

Prayer should never be done by the clock. It should never be looked upon as an obligation, a required work, or a duty.

Remember, the length of your prayer isn't important. Often, there just isn't enough time for lengthy prayers. For instance, suppose your car is stalled on the railroad tracks and the train is heading your way. If it takes a long prayer to do the job—you've had it!

Jesus warned us, "And when you pray, do not use vain repetitions as the heathen do. For they think that they will be heard for their many words" (Matthew 6:7).

Many people criticize the Catholics for their repetitious use of *Hail Mary's* and *Our Father's*. But continually repeating, "Jesus! Jesus!" or "Glory! Glory!" or any other phrase, with no real meaning or intent, is also using vain repetition. If a person came up to me and spoke to me with vain repetition—just speaking a lot of words over and over—I would think, "What is wrong with them?" But some people think nothing of speaking like that to God. "Hallelujah, hallelujah, hallelujah, hallelujah. Oh, bless God, bless God, bless Him, bless God. Hallelujah, hallelujah. Praise God, bless God, bless Him, hallelujah!" Vain repetition.

When you pray, you are actually talking to the Father and you should talk to Him intelligently. Don't repeat the same words over and over again like a mantra. That will get you nowhere.

## THE REWARD OF PRAYER

Jesus said, "And when you pray, you shall not be like the hypocrites. For they love to pray standing in the synagogues and on the corners of the streets, that they may be seen by men. Assuredly, I say to you, they have their reward" (Matthew 6:5). The word hypocrite in Greek is *hupokrites*. The actors in classical Greek dramas who wore character masks were called *hupokrites*.

In other words, Jesus said, "When you pray, don't be as one who merely puts on an act for the benefit of other people. Don't be as the *hupokrites* who like to pray standing in the synagogues and on street corners to be seen by men."

Some people assume from this Scripture that public prayer is wrong. That is certainly not what Jesus said. Jesus Himself prayed in public. The early church also gathered together for public prayer. The Bible says the believers continued daily "in the apostles' doctrine and fellowship, in the breaking of bread, and in prayers" (Acts 2:42). Clearly, prayer should be an essential part of our gathering together.

But be careful that you are not praying to impress men rather than to communicate to God. This is a real danger especially for ministers, because we pray publicly so often. The real temptation comes at the close of a sermon, when a pastor is tempted to subtly repeat the major points of his message in the closing prayer to make sure the people understood it. Supposedly, we are talking to God, but in actuality, we are trying to bring the point home to the people one more time.

In my early ministry I was almost ruined by public prayer. One day a lady said to me, "You pray the most beautiful prayers." So I thought, *I'll sharpen up on that. I'll make my prayers even more beautiful!* I became so interested in impressing people with the beauty of my prayers that I forgot I was actually talking to the Father. There is a real danger in praying to impress people with how righteous, godly, and spiritually deep you think you are.

## WHICH REWARD DO YOU WANT?

In Matthew 6:5-6, Jesus taught that the motive behind your prayer will result in one of two rewards.

The first reward is one given by men. The man who prays publicly in order to impress people with his spirituality receives his reward when someone says, "Oh, he is so spiritual, so godly!" Watch out for that subtle temptation to draw attention to yourself.

It brings to mind the practice that has developed in some churches where, in the middle of a song, someone stands up while everyone else is sitting. It seems that person is conveniently always right up near the front where they can have the biggest audience. You rarely see people standing up in the back row. They are in a prominent place and they are doing the opposite of what everyone else is doing—they are standing up tall and raising their hands, sometimes swaying back and forth. Aren't they aware that they are drawing attention to themselves? If I were standing up while everybody else was sitting down, I would be self-conscious. Maybe I am more impure than a lot of people, but I know I could not be standing there while everyone else was sitting and *not* have it run through my mind that I hope they all notice how spiritual I am.

People draw attention in other ways—subtle little gestures, or a tone of voice that gives off the impression of holiness. A certain way of nodding, or folding the hands, or turning the head just so— "Oooh, yes, I see." Our flesh just loves to make others think we are righteous.

Watch it! Watch what is in your heart. Be careful that you don't do your righteousness before men to be seen of men. Because if that be the case, you have already received the only reward you are going to get.

The Pharisees were motivated by that public reward. They loved to make a big display of their spirituality. Often, as they made their way to the synagogue, they would stop along the way and say their prayers right there—right in full view of everyone. It was as if they wanted people to see what great spiritual zeal they had—so great, in fact, that it consumed them. "Look, everyone! I'm so holy, I can't even wait until I get to the synagogue to pray!" According to Matthew 6:5, these hypocrites received their reward from the men who praised their show.

That is certainly one option. If you want public applause and a quick reward, you can follow the example of the Pharisees. But the better way, according to Jesus, is to go into your closet, shut the door, and pray to your Father who sees in secret. Then your Father will reward you openly (Matthew 6:6).

The question we must ask ourselves is, "Am I doing this to please man, or to please God?" Motive is everything. You can do the right thing with the wrong motive and completely nullify what you have done. Prayer is wonderful. Fasting is marvelous. But no matter how magnanimous, how generous, how wonderful your action was, if you did it to draw attention to yourself or gain the applause of man, that's all you are going to get.

In the earlier years of my ministry I fasted more often than I do now. And there would be times when I would be fasting, and I would go visit a family and the lady would bring out a cake and offer me a piece. I had two choices at that point: I could decline, telling her I couldn't eat that cake because I was fasting, or I could accept a slice. And so I would eat it. I would take that piece of cake and

I would break my fast. I figured that if I said, "Oh, no, thank you. I can't eat that; I'm fasting," then I would have lost the reward anyhow. So I might as well just go ahead and enjoy the cake.

No matter why you pray, prayer brings rewards. Even false prayers spoken for man's acclamation are rewarding. But from which source do you want your reward—from man, or from God?

## THE PROMISES OF PRAYER

Jesus gave us many fantastic promises regarding prayer.

"Assuredly, I say to you, whatever you bind on earth will be bound in heaven, and whatever you loose on earth will be loosed in heaven. Again I say to you that if two of you agree on earth concerning anything that they ask, it will be done for them by My Father in heaven" (Matthew 18:18–19).

That is a broad and glorious promise!

Jesus also promised, "Have faith in God. For assuredly, I say to you, whoever says to this mountain, 'Be removed and be cast into the sea,' and does not doubt in his heart, but believes that those things he says will be done, he will have whatever he says. Therefore I say to you, whatever things you ask when you pray, believe that you receive them, and you will have them" (Mark 11:22–24).

What a fantastic promise!

Jesus also made this remarkable promise: "And whatever you ask in My name, that I will do, that the Father may be glorified in the Son. If you ask anything in My name, I will do it" (John 14:13–14).

Anything!

Here is another promise: "If you abide in Me, and My words abide in you, you will ask what you desire, and it shall be done for you" (John 15:7).

And yet another: "Whatever you ask the Father in My name, He will give you. Until now you have asked nothing in My name. Ask [the Greek here is *aiteite,* which means "to ask and keep on asking, to beg, to crave or desire"], and you will receive, that your joy may be full" (John 16:23–24).

These are truly amazing promises. The Lord is inviting you to ask Him *anything.* These are broad promises with broad parameters. But to whom were these promises made? Jesus wasn't talking to the multitudes. In every case, Jesus was talking to His disciples.

So who qualifies as a disciple?

Jesus said, "If anyone desires to come after Me, let him deny himself, and take up his cross, and follow Me" (Matthew 16:24). A person who denies himself, takes up his cross daily, and follows Jesus Christ can take these promises and privileges. Anything one asks in Jesus' name will be done.

By virtue of the fact that a disciple has denied himself to follow after Christ, he is not seeking the things that would glorify his flesh. By taking up his cross, he is not seeking his own glory, but reckoning himself to be dead with Christ. His identity is now only in the things that God wants—he has committed himself, his ambitions, and his life totally to Jesus Christ.

The true thrust of a disciple's prayer is always, "Nevertheless, not as I will, but as You will" (Matthew 26:39).

Only by denying yourself, taking up your cross, and following Jesus Christ do you receive access to the powerful promises of God regarding your prayers.

## GOD WANTS TO BLESS YOU THROUGH PRAYER

When King Asa first came to the throne, he faced a very difficult situation. He had a good-sized army—some 580,000 men who bore shields and bows—but the Ethiopians had invaded the land with a million-man army and 300 chariots. In those days, a chariot was equivalent to a tank in modern warfare. And an infantry just doesn't do very well against tanks.

Asa knew there was no way he could defend his nation from this huge invading army and their chariots. So King Asa did something wise: he cried out to God. That is the best thing to do when you face an impossible task. Man's extremities are God's opportunities. When we have exhausted our store of endurance, that is when God shows Himself mighty on our behalf.

The first thing Asa did was to acknowledge God's greatness and His power. "LORD, it is nothing for You to help, whether with many or with those who have no power ... " (2 Chronicles 14:11). Asa knew that though the odds against him surviving were great, those odds meant nothing at all to God. If God be for us, who can be against us? It only takes two to make a majority—God and you.

Asa then said, " ... help us, O LORD our God; for we rest on You...." He took it a step further. Not only is Asa trusting God with the problem, he is trusting Him so completely that he is able to rest in the outcome. That reminds me of a stanza from the old song, *I am His, and He is Mine*:

> *Things that once were wild alarms cannot*
>     *now disturb my rest;*
> *Closed in everlasting arms, pillowed on the*
>     *loving breast.*
> *O to lie forever here, doubt and care and*
>     *self resign,*
> *While He whispers in my ear, I am His,*
>     *and He is mine.* [1]

---

[1] *I Am His and He is Mine*, Robinson, George W., copyright 1876.

Once you give a problem to God, leave it there with Him. If we continue to worry about it, that indicates that we don't really trust Him with it.

" ... and in Your name we go against this multitude." It is important to go out in the name of the Lord and in His strength—not in our own.

"O LORD, You are our God; do not let man prevail against You!" Note that Asa didn't say, "Do not let man prevail against us!" That is because Asa understood that the battle belonged to God. It was His reputation at stake, not theirs. "We are right behind You, Lord!" Asa was saying. And that is a good place to be. We don't want to be in front—we want the Lord to be in front of us.

God heard Asa's prayer. When Asa and his hopelessly outnumbered, outgunned army went forward to meet the enemy, the Lord went with them—and they destroyed the Ethiopian army.

When King Asa returned from victory, the prophet Azariah met him and said, "The LORD is with you while you are with Him. If you seek Him, He will be found by you; but if you forsake Him, He will forsake you" (2 Chronicles 15:2).

After this, Asa began to prosper and became very strong and powerful. In the latter years of his reign, he was threatened yet again. But this time, the threat came from Baasha, the king of the northern tribes of Israel, who was building fortified cities north of Jerusalem in preparation for an invasion. This time, Asa didn't stop to pray. Instead, he took money out of the treasury and sent it to hire Ben-Hadad, the king of Syria, to invade Israel from the north. This caused Baasha to withdraw his troops from invading Judah and to deploy them to defend the northern border. It was a clever strategy, and it worked.

Asa had not sought the Lord. Rather, he sought human help. Because of that, the prophet Hanani came to Asa and rebuked him. The prophet reminded him of how the Lord had helped him against the Ethiopians at the beginning of his reign, and then Hanani declared, "For the eyes of the LORD run to and fro throughout the whole earth, to show Himself strong on behalf of those whose heart is loyal to Him" (2 Chronicles 16:9).

Here is a basic truth about God: He is looking for people to bless. I hope you let that truth sink into your heart. Really meditate on it. God wants to work in your life and He wants to bless you. He wants to use you as one of His instruments, but He is waiting for you to come into alignment with His plan. The moment your life comes into harmony with the purposes of God, you become a channel through which God's power and love can flow to a needy world.

God is looking for people whose hearts are in tune with His desires. Thus, the best prayer we can utter is, "Lord, bring me into harmony with Your will." You can't improve on that. But it has to be more than just lip service. It has to come from the heart.

What a privilege it is to be able to enter into the presence of God with just an uttered prayer. It is a privilege to have God share His desires with you and plant His will within your heart. And it is a privilege to be used by God to minister to a needy world. God promises to do all of that and more—if you will ask Him.

CHAPTER 10

# Prayer in Action

The Bible teaches that faith produces answered prayer. Jesus said, "Therefore I say to you, whatever things you ask when you pray, believe that you receive them, and you will have them" (Mark 11:24).

It is much easier to have faith for answered prayers when you realize the magnificent power of the One to whom you are talking. In the book of Acts the disciples prayed, "Lord, You are God, who made heaven and earth and the sea, and all that is in them" (Acts 4:24). The disciples were well aware of the power Jesus possessed. They knew the God to whom they were talking.

## GOD IS ABLE TO ACT AND ANSWER

One thing that hinders our faith is that we have a tendency

to ascribe our own limitations to God. It's as if we forget that the One we are speaking to is the Creator of the universe. But He's not like us. He is not limited by our abilities. Nothing restricts or hinders Him—unlike us.

Sometimes we know just enough about the circumstances of our situation that we have trouble praying with faith. For example, I have a mechanical mind. Therefore, it is difficult for me to pray for a miracle when the engine in my car won't run. Because I know quite well that the coil is weak, the points are bad, and the battery has been run down, I lack the faith needed to pray. It just doesn't occur to me to pray, "Oh God, help this car to start!"

However, my wife doesn't know a thing about mechanics. She has rarely looked under the hood of a car. She doesn't know a distributor from a carburetor, or an oil dipstick from a radiator cap. So she can have great faith whenever we have trouble getting the car started.

I'll tell her, "That's it. The car is shot."

And she will say, "Let's pray."

I'll answer, "Aw, come on! We can't pray for something like this. It's mechanical."

But she will bow her head and say, "Lord, help this car to start now. You know we have got to get going. I thank You, Father, and I ask it in Jesus' name." Then she'll say, "Okay. Try it again."

I'll say, "But it's no use!"

"Just go ahead and try it."

And you know what happens? The engine fires right up!

The next time you think, "What's the use of praying?" Look around the universe at what God has already done. Then figure out what His limitations might be.

He is quite a big God, you know. Yet we sometimes pray as if we were talking to someone extremely limited in power. "Oh Lord! I don't know if You can do this or not. I even hate to ask You; and if You can't, well, that's all right. I understand."

The difficulty of a task must always be measured by the capacity of the agent called upon to do the work. Who is the agent you are calling upon? You are calling on the Lord God Almighty, the Creator of the universe, the Creator of *you*. You are calling on your heavenly Father, the One who loves you and cares deeply about the details of your life. And as the LORD asked Abraham in Genesis 18:14, "Is anything too hard for the LORD?" The answer, of course, is no. There is nothing too hard for God.

If it helps, begin your prayer with an acknowledgment of God's great strength and power. Jeremiah did this. "Ah, Lord God! Behold, You have made the heavens and the earth by Your great power and outstretched arm. There is nothing too hard for You" (Jeremiah 32:17). Jeremiah didn't need to remind God of His great power. I suspect he was reminding himself.

It is vital in prayer that we recognize the greatness of God. David knew this. He said, "When I consider Your heavens, the work of Your fingers, the moon and the stars, which You have ordained, what is man that You are mindful of him?" (Psalm 8:3-4). David looked up at the stars, and he saw the greatness of God.

Unfortunately, living in this urban society, we rarely get a chance to view the heavens. We have light pollution. We have air pollution. It used to be that you could go out in the desert to get a good look at the heavens, but even in the desert now there is a certain amount of air and light pollution. So you don't see that clearly anymore. I can remember, though, as a child, the brightness of the stars at night. How I would look up and see the Milky Way. You can't help but be impressed by the vastness of the universe—and the God who created it.

One thing David didn't have was the specific information we now know about the universe. He didn't know that our planet is 8,000 miles in diameter and 25,000 miles in circumference at the equator. He didn't know that the earth revolves around the sun every 365 days, six hours, nine minutes and nine fifty-fourths of a second—right on time, year in and year out. Nor did he know that the sun around which our earth rotates is 1,200,000 times larger than the earth in volume, 865,000 miles in circumference; and that if you could hollow out the sun, leaving a crust of 100,000 miles, you could put the earth inside of the sun and let the moon rotate around the earth and you would still have close to a hundred thousand miles to spare.

David didn't have that specific information, but he did have the heavens. I am certain that as he stood under that great, vast night sky, looking out at the universe, he was awed by the greatness of God. "When I consider Your heavens, the work of Your fingers, the moon and the stars, which You have ordained … "

You need that same awareness of God's power and majesty. You need to remember that the God who created this great, big universe is the God who has made Himself available to you, to help you in the greatest problems of life that you might face. Otherwise, you won't have the faith to transfer your burden to Him.

Now, many times, by the time we pray about our situation, we have been carrying it on our shoulders for awhile. It feels like a thousand tons. Overwhelmed, we pray, "Oh Lord, what can possibly move this mountain? You know what the doctor said about this, Lord. It is fatal in 99% of the cases. Oh Lord, this is horrible, just horrible!"

We are so weighed down with the problem that we have forgotten we are talking with the One who created the heavens, the earth, the sea, and everything that is in them. It is no more difficult for God to cure a person in the last stages of leukemia than it is for Him to take away a sore throat. It is no more difficult for God to put a new arm on a man than it is to remove his headache.

You may say, "Come on, now. There are limits."

What if a starfish lost one of its arms? Would you have a hard time praying, "God, put a new arm on that starfish?" No. We know that nature causes a new arm to grow on a starfish. Cut a little earthworm in half, and nature will make it grow another half. But what is nature? Who created the laws of nature? Could not God, who created us, and all the functions within us, cause a new arm to grow? If He can put within the earthworm the capacity to grow another half, why would it be difficult for Him to put a new arm or a new leg on a person?

When we think of such miracles, our limited human understanding stymies us, and we carry that limitation over to God. "Don't bother about a new arm, God," we say. "Just help him adjust to living without it."

Sometimes God will perform miracles just to show us He can do it—in spite of our unbelief.

When I was pastoring in Tucson, a lady named June called me one day and said, "Oh, Chuck, pray for my little son, David. The car door slammed on his finger. We are at the doctor's office and he says he will have to amputate! Please pray, Chuck, that God will heal it, and they won't have to amputate David's finger."

I began praying with June over the phone. The Spirit moved upon my heart and I really felt hopeful about the situation. At the end of our prayer, I told her, "I believe

God is going to heal David's finger! Praise the Lord and rejoice! God is going to do a miraculous work!"

The doctor told David's mother, "Bring him back tomorrow, and we'll decide then if we have to amputate."

The next day she took little David back to the specialist. He looked at the finger and said, "I'm sorry, but blood poisoning has already set in. I'm going to have to amputate. The bone is crushed and there is nothing else I can do."

June called me on the phone. She was crying so hard she couldn't talk.

"What's the matter?" I asked.

But she couldn't answer me. Her sister finally took the phone and said, "Chuck, the doctor just amputated the tip of David's finger and it has June completely shaken."

I said, "Tell her I'll meet her at the house."

As I drove to her house, I began to question God. "Lord," I said, "why didn't You heal that finger? You could have healed it so easily! That's nothing for You. I told her to trust and have faith in You. Now I have got to go and talk to her. She is hysterical, and I don't know what to say!"

When I got to her house, I said, "June, we know that all things work together for good to them that love God. God has a purpose. It could have been his whole finger, or an arm. Be thankful it was just the tip of the finger. David will learn to adjust, and someday we'll discover God's purposes."

It is not easy to counsel in these situations, but I did the best I could. On my way home I continued to question God. "Lord, I just don't understand what You are doing! If I were You, I certainly would have healed that finger."

The incident shook my faith. In fact, I doubt I could have prayed for someone's cold that night. The faith of David's mother was shattered. Though I tried to comfort her, she couldn't be comforted.

But the next morning she called me. She was very excited, screaming on the phone, "Chuck! Chuck! Something happened!"

"What now?" I said.

"It's fabulous!" she said. "David was wrestling with his brother and he knocked the bandage off his finger. I went to put the bandage back on—and there is another whole pink fingertip growing out! It looks like brand new flesh!" She took David to the specialist who looked at the finger and scratched his head. "Nurse, bring me my chart," he said. He read the chart over a few times and then said, "Nurse, we did amputate, didn't we?"

"Yes, doctor," she said.

The doctor shook his head, clearly perplexed. "That's impossible!" he said. Then he asked David's mother, "Could you bring David back tomorrow, please?"

His mother brought David the next day and the doctor went through the same routine—still stunned and perplexed. "Would you mind bringing him back again tomorrow?" he said.

Every day for a week David's mother had to bring her little boy into the specialist, who did little more than read his chart and look at David's new fingertip and scratch his head. Finally, he x-rayed the fingertip and discovered that the bone was intact. He said, "This is something amazing! As far as I know, medical science has never seen anything like this. I have no explanation for it at all."

Then he turned to June. "Of course, you realize that David will never have a nail on that fingertip. It is impossible for a new nail to ever form."

I wonder if God took those words as a dare. A couple of weeks later, a fingernail began growing. Within two months David could hold out both hands, and you couldn't tell which fingertip had been amputated!

David went back to the doctor once a week for a year. The doctor took pictures, documented the whole event and submitted it to the Journal of the American Medical Association. The doctor was Jewish, and David's mother testified to him about the power of Jesus Christ. He finally said, "I have to confess that this is a miracle of God."

I thought about what I had asked God when David first got hurt—how I had prayed and asked Him to heal David's finger, and I realized that had God healed the finger before the amputation, the specialist would never have believed any part of the mother's witness. He would have rationalized that the body healed itself. But after the amputation? "Lord, You are so smart!" I said. "You did this to amaze that doctor, didn't You?"

When we find ourselves facing a challenge, why do we doubt God? Why do we limit Him? We do it because *we* are limited, and because we forget to look up and remember to whom we are talking when we pray. The best thing we can do is to stop looking at the mountain in front of us and start looking at the One who created all things—and the One who has the power to get us up and over that mountain.

## CHAPTER 11

# God's Kingdom Come

Most of us are familiar with the Lord's Prayer. How many times do you suppose you have prayed, "Your kingdom come. Your will be done on earth as it is in heaven"? That is probably one of the best-known and most-repeated prayers in the world. But what exactly are you praying for when you repeat those words?

Whether we realize what we are saying or not, that line of the Lord's Prayer is an acknowledgment of the fact that at the present time, God's kingdom is not on earth. It is interesting—God created the whole universe, and this one small part of the universe, the one called earth, is in rebellion against God and against His authority.

In the parable of the talents, Jesus tells of a certain noble-man and describes the attitude his servants had toward him. They hated their master, Jesus said, and declared, "We will not have this man to reign over us" (Luke 19:12-14).

That is pretty much the attitude of the world today: "We will not have this Man to rule over us." But when we pray, "Your kingdom come. Your will be done on earth as it is in heaven," we are praying that Jesus *will* rule over us. We are expressing a longing for His return. Those of us who belong to Jesus long for Him to rule over the world in which we live, and we look in anticipation for that day.

## THE WORLD GOD PLANNED; THE WORLD WE INHERITED

The present world is in rebellion against God. For now, the kingdom of darkness and death rules the earth. The world we see today is not the world that God created. The world God created was perfect. When you read through the six days of creation, you see that day by day, as God surveyed that which He had created, He declared it to be good. After God created this beautiful world—and we can only wonder at how perfect and unsullied it must have been—He then created man to inhabit the earth. But something happened that marred the good world God created—sin entered the picture.

God had given Adam and Eve great liberty there in the garden of Eden. He told them they were free to eat of all the trees in the garden, with the exception of one tree, the tree of the knowledge of good and evil. They were not to eat of that one tree. God warned that in the day they did, they would surely die. Of course, we know the story. Adam and Eve did disobey God. They listened to Satan's lie that perhaps God had not really said they would die. They gave in to the temptation; and as a consequence, Paul tells us that "through one man, sin entered the world, and death through sin; and thus death spread to all men" (Romans 5:12).

In Genesis chapter 3, God announced to Adam and Eve the consequences of their sin. Disobedience to God always brings consequences. You can't escape it. God's laws are set. If you violate them you will suffer for it. It isn't that God is saying, "You did that to Me, so now I'm going to do this to you." It is just innate within the action of sin itself.

It is interesting that people so often view the law of God as being restrictive. They think, "God doesn't want me to have any fun. His law just binds me and holds me back." But isn't that exactly what Satan said to Eve? "For God knows that in the day you eat of it your eyes will be opened, and you will be like God, knowing good and evil" (Genesis 3:5). Satan wanted Eve to think that God was holding back something good from her.

And that is what Satan wants us to think. As often as he can, he tries to suggest to us that God is holding us back from that which is good and pleasurable. But that is a lie. God has never forbidden that which is good. He only forbids those things that will bring negative consequences into our lives. Because He can look ahead and see the misery and pain sin will bring you, He wants to protect you and spare you from that suffering. And so, in His goodness, He forbids that which is dangerous to you. You can trust His law. You can believe that it is good and right, and meant for your protection. As the psalmist said, "The law of the LORD is perfect, converting the soul; the testimony of the LORD is sure, making wise the simple; the statutes of the LORD are right, rejoicing the heart; the commandment of the LORD is pure, enlightening the eyes" (Psalms 19:7-8).

Because Adam and Eve believed Satan's lies and disobeyed the commandment of God, they brought upon the world all of the sorrow, all of the misery, and all of the pain we see today. God would have spared us death. I believe that God, when He created our bodies, created them perfectly. Just look at how the cells of the body recreate themselves every seven years! Think about how this process could have gone on and on and on, and you would have stayed forever young, forever healthy, forever in a perfect body. Sin brought the aging process. The mutating of the cells, the breakdown of the cells—all those things that cause aging didn't need to happen. That was not God's intention for us.

The beautiful world God created produced an abundance of all kinds of fruit and nuts and vegetables. Man did not even have to cultivate the ground. All he had to do was go out and pick whatever he wanted and just enjoy it. And within the food were all the nutrients needed for man to maintain perfect health.

In the beginning there was perfect climate. I don't think we had the north or south poles with their great ice packs. I think the earth had a different degree in its axis. Today it is tilted at twenty-three-and-a-third degrees, but I think the axis was different in the original world God created. We know that in the Arctic Circle, they have found the frozen remains of great mammoths up in the tundra of Siberia. Within the digestive tracts of these mammals they found tropical vegetation, which means that the geographical structure of the earth was much different than it is today. In the South Pole, great charcoal deposits have been found two hundred feet below the ice, indicating there had once been a vast forest in that region. It would seem that at one time there was moderate climate all over the earth, without the violent storms or hurricanes we see so much today.

But the curse of sin changed the world. What we see today isn't the way God first created the world. We probably can't even imagine how beautiful the world was back when it was fresh and untouched.

Most of us appreciate places where nature is more or less undisturbed—places where man has not yet marred it with his touch. It is wonderful to get away for a walk or a hike and leave civilization behind. We take in a big breath and look around at the pristine beauty of untouched nature—and we love it. But the fact is, no matter how remote the area, no matter how far we hike, the beauty we see does not even come close to the beauty God originally created. Because Adam and Eve rebelled against God's laws, and mankind throughout history has continued to rebel against God's laws, we suffer the consequences of that rebellion. Because of sin, we have lost the beauty of the world God created for us. Instead, we are living in a fallen world.

The world God intended was perfect. This world, however, contains thorns and thistles and noxious weeds. This world requires that a man work to eat, whereas God intended our work to be limited to reaching up and plucking a piece of ripe fruit from a tree. This world is filled with all manner of sickness and disease, aging and death. This world is filled with turmoil, strife, wars, murders, fighting, and sorrow.

## HOPE

It makes you weary, doesn't it? Sorrow and suffering have that effect. But throughout the Bible, God has promised weary man—those emotionally torn because of sin's consequences—a day coming when the earth would be restored according to its original beauty and glory. He promised also to restore man to His original intent. The day is coming when we will see the world as God intended it to be. That time is known in the Scriptures as the kingdom age, and that is what we are praying for when we pray, "Your kingdom come. Your will be done on earth as it is in heaven."

The first issue that will have to be dealt with is the issue that has caused all the pain, sorrow, and suffering in our world—the issue of sin. As long as sin exists, we will continue to suffer from disease, aging, turmoil, and death. So God has to go straight to the heart of the problem—He has to deal with the issue of sin first. That was the purpose of the first coming of Jesus. He came to deal directly with sin.

Because of the sacrifice of Christ, you and I can experience the forgiveness and the cleansing of sin. Because our sins have been paid and we have been justified through our faith in Jesus Christ, we can enjoy fellowship with God.

Unfortunately, we are still living in a sinful world. We can't escape that yet. But when we pray, "Your kingdom come. Your will be done on earth as it is in heaven," we are actually praying for that day when sin will be abolished and all men will live together as God intended—in love and in peace.

God is presently gathering from among the world those people who desire to see His kingdom come—citizens for that coming kingdom. The Holy Spirit is at work in the world, gathering together people who want to surrender their will and their lives to God and to live as God intended for them to live. If you have received Jesus Christ, you have been marked for God's kingdom. And when that day comes and His will is being done here on earth, you will share in that glorious kingdom that Jesus establishes.

## GOD'S COMING WORLD

The day is coming—and I am convinced it is not far off—when Jesus is coming to rule and reign over the earth. He will establish God's righteous kingdom, and that kingdom will extend over the whole world. Today, obedience to God's laws is optional. You have a choice: you can obey God's commandments, or you can ignore them and go your own way. But when Jesus establishes His kingdom, it will no longer be optional. On that day, you will either abide by God's laws or you will be forced to leave the kingdom.

The Bible is clear about that. God's Word has much to say about the coming kingdom and about how it relates to Jesus. In fact, as we look through the following Scriptures, you will see that this coming kingdom is the general theme of God's Word. Everything is pointing toward that wonderful day when the kingdom of God is established on the earth.

**LUKE 1:33** identifies Jesus as the One who will rule and reign forever. When the angel visited Mary, he told her, concerning the Child she was to bring into the world, "He will reign over the house of Jacob forever; and of His kingdom there shall be no end."

**REVELATION 19:16** tells us about the supremacy of Jesus Christ, visible to all as He comes to take His reign. "And He has on His robe and on His thigh a name written: KING OF KINGS AND LORD OF LORDS."

**PHILIPPIANS 2:5-11** says that although today men reject Jesus and blaspheme His name, in that day, there will be no dispute about who reigns over the earth—no ignoring of God's Son, no taking His name in vain. All will recognize and acknowledge Jesus as Lord. "Let this mind be in you which was also in Christ Jesus, who, being in the form of God, did not consider it robbery to be equal with God, but made Himself of no reputation, taking the form of a bond-servant, and coming in the likeness of men. And being found in appearance as a man, He humbled Himself and became obedient to the point of death, even the death of the cross. Therefore God also has highly exalted Him and given Him the name which is above every name, that at the name of Jesus every knee should bow, of those in heaven, and of those on earth, and of those under the earth, and that every tongue should confess that Jesus Christ is Lord, to the glory of God the Father."

**MALACHI 1:11** also speaks about the honor that will be given to the name of Jesus. "'For from the rising of the sun, even to its going down, My name shall be great among the Gentiles; in every place incense shall be offered to My name, and a pure offering; for My name shall be great among the nations,' says the LORD of hosts."

**PSALM 2:7** proclaims that the coming kingdom is Jesus' inheritance. "I will declare the decree: The LORD has said to Me, 'You are My Son, today I have begotten You. Ask of Me, and I will give You the nations for Your inheritance, and the ends of the earth for Your possession" (Psalm 2:7-8).

These verses from Psalms reveal that the reign of Jesus Christ will be a universal reign. "All the ends of the world shall remember and turn to the LORD, and all the families of the nations shall worship before You. For the kingdom is the LORD's, and He rules over the nations" (Psalm 22:27-28). "Yes, all kings shall fall down before Him; all nations shall serve Him" (Psalm 72:11). "All nations whom You have made shall come and worship before You, O Lord, and shall glorify Your name" (Psalm 86:9).

REVELATION 11:15 assures us that the coming kingdom will be the final kingdom—the eternal kingdom. "And there were loud voices in heaven, saying, 'The kingdoms of this world have become the kingdoms of our Lord and of His Christ, and He shall reign forever and ever!'"

EXODUS 15:18 declares, "The LORD shall reign forever and ever."

HEBREWS 1:8 sets forth that the coming kingdom will be righteous. "Your throne, O God, is forever and ever; a scepter of righteousness is the scepter of Your Kingdom."

DANIEL 2:44 promises that this coming kingdom will be indestructible. "And in the days of these kings the God of heaven will set up a kingdom which shall never be destroyed; and the kingdom shall not be left to other people; it shall break in pieces and consume all these kingdoms, and it shall stand forever."

The "kings" mentioned in this verse are the ten rulers of the European Community. We see Europe rising now as a world-dominating power. That is why I believe we are not very far from the answer to our prayers, "Your kingdom come. Your will be done on earth as it is in heaven."

ISAIAH 9:7, 11:6 say that the reign of Jesus Christ will be a reign of eternal peace. "Of the increase of His government and peace there will be no end, upon the throne of David and over His kingdom, to order it and establish it with judgment and justice from that time forward, even forever. The zeal of the LORD of hosts will perform this ... The wolf also shall dwell with the lamb, the leopard will lie down with the young goat, the calf and the young lion and the fatling together; and a little child shall lead them. The cow and the bear shall graze; their young ones shall lie down together; and the lion shall eat straw like an ox. The nursing child shall play by the cobra's hole, and the weaned child shall put his hand in the viper's den. They shall not hurt nor destroy in all My holy mountain, for the earth shall be full of the knowledge of the LORD as the waters cover the sea."

MICAH 4:1-4 confirms that Jesus will reign in peace, and it tells us that Jesus will rule from Jerusalem. "Now it shall come to pass in the latter days that the mountain of the LORD's house shall be established on the top of the mountains, and shall be exalted above the hills; and peoples shall flow to it. Many nations shall come and say, 'Come, and let us go up to the mountain of the LORD, to the house of the God of Jacob; He will teach us His ways, and we shall walk in His paths.' For out of Zion the law shall go forth, and the word of the LORD from Jerusalem. He shall judge between many peoples, and rebuke strong nations afar off; they shall beat their swords into plowshares, and their spears into pruning hooks; nation shall not lift up sword against nation, neither shall they learn war anymore. But everyone shall sit under his vine and under his fig tree, and no one shall make them afraid; for the mouth of the LORD of hosts has spoken."

What a glorious day that will be—when men will turn their weapons of warfare into farming tools! The billions that would have been spent arming ourselves with weapons can instead be used to develop the earth's agricultural resources.

**DANIEL 7:18, 22, 27** tell us that Jesus will share His kingdom with us. "But the saints of the Most High shall receive the kingdom, and possess the kingdom forever, even forever and ever ... until the Ancient of Days came, and a judgment was made in favor of the saints of the Most High, and the time came for the saints to possess the kingdom. 'Then the kingdom and dominion, and the greatness of the kingdoms under the whole heaven, shall be given to the people, the saints of the Most High. His kingdom is an everlasting kingdom, and all dominions shall serve and obey Him.'"

**ISAIAH 35:1-7, 9-10 (KJV)** gives us a preview of the incredible changes God will bring upon the earth when Jesus comes to reign in the new kingdom. "The desert shall rejoice, and blossom as the rose. It shall blossom abundantly, and rejoice even with joy and singing: the glory of Lebanon shall be given unto it, the excellency of Carmel and Sharon, they shall see the glory of the LORD, and the excellency of our God. Strengthen ye the weak hands, and confirm the feeble knees. Say to them that are of a fearful heart, Be strong, fear not: behold, your God will come with vengeance, even God with a recompence; He will come and save you. Then the eyes of the blind shall be opened, the ears of the deaf shall be unstopped. Then shall the lame man leap as a hart, and the tongue of the dumb sing: for in the wilderness shall waters break out, and streams in the desert. And the parched ground shall become a pool, and the thirsty land springs of water ... no lion shall be there, nor any ravenous beast shall go up thereon, it shall not be found there; but the redeemed shall walk there: and the ransomed of the LORD shall return, and come to Zion with songs and everlasting joy upon their heads: they shall obtain joy and gladness, and sorrow and sighing shall flee away."

Did you catch what God is promising in this passage? He is promising to make all things new. He is promising to restore the earth to its original beauty, and remove—forever—the marks of sin.

Oh, that He would come today! How wonderful it will be when God's kingdom is established and He takes His rightful place as Ruler over the earth! Surely, in light of those marvelous promises, our hearts long for that day. Surrounded as we are by misery, pain, and suffering, the promise of His kingdom only fuels the intensity of our prayer: "Your kingdom come. Your will be done on earth as it is in heaven."

Come quickly, Lord Jesus.

## CHAPTER 12

# ARE YOU READY?

The question of who wins the battle between God and Satan has already been answered: God wins. The question of what happens to the earth after the tribulation period has already been answered: Jesus will return to establish God's kingdom. Only one question remains: When He returns, will you be ready?

Some of you are ready right now. You have confessed Jesus Christ as your Lord and you have accepted the rule of Christ over your life. If He rules your life, you can be sure that you are ready for the coming kingdom of God. While you wait, of course, you still have to live in the world. You are still subject to the sorrows and miseries that sin has brought upon the earth. But the day is coming when the Lord will take His church out of this world, and when He returns with His church to rule and reign over the earth, you will return with Him.

But some of you reading this book are not ready for God's kingdom. You are those Jesus spoke about in Luke 19:14, who said, "We will not have this Man to reign over us." Because you live for yourself and your pleasures, and believe you know best how you should live, you refuse to surrender your life to Jesus Christ.

I want to take this last opportunity to clear up a misconception you may have about God's laws. The very rules you balk at, the rules you seek to bend or break or ignore, are rules God has given for your protection. They are rules He has given to keep you from hurting yourself. You can go on violating God's laws, but if you choose to do so, you have no one to blame for the resulting pain but yourself. You can't blame God for the consequences of your choice. You can't ignore the help He freely offers and then blame Him for the calamities that come into your life.

Years ago, when I was pastoring a church in Tucson, a woman visited one Sunday whose husband was a captain in the U.S. Air Force. At that time we made a habit of visiting the families of those who came to church, so I went to visit their home. The husband answered the door and I introduced myself. When I told him I was the pastor of the church his wife had attended the previous Sunday, the man began cursing me and ordered me off of his property.

"My little girl that you met last Sunday—the little girl in the wheelchair? Her crippled body is the result of polio. And now," he said, "the doctor tells me my second daughter has polio. I want nothing to do with your God!"

His reaction was violent and his language horrible. I said to him, "Sir, have you been serving God?" Of course, he became very angry at that. He made it clear that he wasn't serving God and he never would.

I said, "Well, if you are not serving God, how is it that you want and expect God to protect your family and watch over you? You are ready to blame God for the tragedies in your life, but why? If you are not God's servant, what do you think He owes you?"

That was the end of our conversation, unfortunately. He insisted that I leave, and I did so. I left feeling very sad. That man was no different from a great many people who refuse to surrender their lives to God, yet expect Him to guide and protect them. Though they ignore God regularly, they are quick to point at Him and blame Him each time a problem comes into their lives. I am not saying that those who serve and follow God will never experience tragedy. But I am saying that those who reject God should not be angry when the path they have chosen proves to be difficult. And I am saying that those who follow God can rest in the knowledge that the troubles they face are troubles God has permitted for their growth. We can rest knowing that God will use those things to accomplish His purposes in our lives.

I urge you to ready yourself for the coming kingdom—for it is surely coming, and coming soon. Surrender your life to Jesus Christ today. He loves you more than you know, and He wants to bless your life. As He says through Jeremiah, "'For I know the thoughts that I think toward you,' says the LORD, 'thoughts of peace and not of evil, to give you a future and a hope'" (Jeremiah 29:11).

A future and a hope—blessing upon blessing. Let God give you that future and that hope today.

In concluding a book on prayer, it is only right and reasonable that I take this opportunity to pray for you.

> *Father, I pray that You will draw the one reading this book to Yourself. I ask that You will remind this one that the world in which we live is not our permanent dwelling place. Help us to keep our eyes on You, and to keep our thoughts on heaven—our true home. When trouble comes, help us to trust that You are working out Your purposes for us.*
>
> *Lord, we ask Your forgiveness for the times when we have taken Your gift of prayer for granted. Oh, what a glorious privilege it is to speak to You, to be able to enter into Your presence at any moment and share our hearts with You! Teach us to pray more, Father—to pray continually. Give us a desire to commune*

*with You. Build in us an urgency to pray for our world, our nation, our cities, our families. Align our will with Yours. Have Your way with us, Lord. We are Your servants.*

*And Lord, may we use this glorious privilege of prayer each day to hasten Your coming. May Your kingdom come, Your will be done on earth as it is in heaven.*

*In Jesus' name, amen.*